Shakespeare
The Director's Cut
Volume 2

Shakespeare
The Director's Cut
Volume 2

The Histories

Michael
Bogdanov

Capercaillie Books

CAPERCAILLIE BOOKS LIMITED

First published by Capercaillie Books Limited in 2005

Registered Office 1 Rutland Court, Edinburgh

© Michael Bogdanov

The moral rights of the author have been asserted.

Design by Ian Kirkwood Design.

Printed in Poland.

Typeset by Chimera Creations in Cosmos and Veljovic.

A catalogue record of this book is available from the British Library

Hardback ISBN 0-9545206-8-8
Paperback ISBN 0-9549625-9-1

To Sue Evans, whose unflagging enthusiasm and loyalty sustained the English Shakespeare Company through twelve exhilarating years.

Contents

Introduction

The world of Shakespeare is one of a continual power struggle – action versus inaction. The power of the imagination versus *real politik*. The pragmatic versus the creative. From beginning to end Shakespeare was obsessed with the discrepancy between the thought of action and the act itself. The power of the mind to conceive of systems, universes, utopias, versus the gulf that exists between these dreams and the reality of coping with the environmental, cultural and economic disaster that is engulfing the world at this moment with ever greater rapidity. Greed, avarice, war, aggression, slaughter in God's name. Richmond in *Richard III* – God give me strength in my right arm (sic), to kill as many of my enemies as possible. It takes a butcher to beat a butcher. Bolingbroke's dying advice to Hal – 'Busy giddy minds with foreign quarrels'. Get out there, son, and deflect the country's attention away from the problems of unemployment, taxation, homelessness, with a 'just' war, trumped up by the Church against the French. Nearly six hundred years later Thatcher triumphed domestically the same way, the Archbishop blessing the troops at Plymouth as they left for the Falklands. Richard III, the man who says, 'That's what I'm going to do', and does it. Claudius and Hamlet, two men caught midway between the thought of action and the act itself. The one starting as man of action, the other finishing. In the middle, meeting in indeterminate indecision. Prospero, the man for whom it all happens in his head. He may conceive of overturning the natural order, reverse the laws of the universe, plan revolutionary systems, humble and humiliate his enemies, but at the end of it all, he will wake up, get up from his café table, pay for his croissant and his coffee and wander off down the street, exactly the same as when he started.

How to rule without being a ruthless pragmatist? Is it possible? Why can good government not encompass imagination and humanity? Why must it always consist of inhuman decisions to combat inhuman situations? As Alcibiades says in *Timon of Athens* when he comes storming in (another usurper) – 'I shall use the olive with the sword'. The problem is, how much olive, how much sword? Once force is used, where does it stop? Violent ends and violent means. The lessons of history continually unlearnt, as the West is finding to its cost in Afghanistan and Iraq.

Shakespeare poses a status quo, one against which he pits a protagonist. This protagonist usually smashes him or herself to pieces on the rock of the state, temporarily turning the turtle over on its back, before the turtle rights itself again and rumbles on its reactionary way. The tentacles of state bind protectively round the body of society, Rosencrantz and Guildenstern's 'massey wheel'. What lessons have been learnt? What has changed? The pyramid of power remains intact. The territorial imperative is exercised once again in the name of justice, divine right, necessity of state, etc . . . Pragmatism. *Real politik*. As Bolingbroke says in *Henry IV, Part 1*, 'If these things be necessities, let us treat them like necessities'. Blair should play the part. What am I talking about? He already does. Which brings me to The Wars of the Roses.

* * *

In Spring 1986, Michael Pennington and I sat in a coffee bar around the corner from the Arts Council of Great Britain in Piccadilly and plotted the downfall of the acceptable face of British theatre. Our plan was to launch a radical alternative to the Royal Shakespeare Company by producing highly politicised versions of *Henry IV, Parts 1* and *2*, and *Henry V* with a company of 25 actors, and tour them all round Britain, performing all three plays every Saturday. We called the project 'The Henrys'. The Arts Council jumped at the idea.

The following year, going for broke, (in all senses) we added *Richard II*, the three *Henry VIs* condensed into two parts – entitled The House of Lancaster and The House of York – and *Richard III*, and toured world wide for two years under the banner of 'The Wars of the Roses'. On numerous occasions we played all seven in a week-end – *Richard II* on Friday night, *The Henry IVs* and *Henry V* on Saturday, The *Henry VIs* and *Richard III* on Sunday – a total of twenty four hours of Shakespeare out of fifty two. A plan to perform them all consecutively with only an hour and a half between each play never came to fruition.

How did it all come about?

I had been doing mediocre work at The Royal National Theatre where I was an Associate Director from 1980 – 1988. After an initial burst of success (and controversy with *The Romans in Britain*), I was unable to break a run of productions that seemed indistinguishable from A Thousand and One Anonymous Nights that (dis)graced the English stage. A limited success with Alfred de Musset's *Lorenzaccio* (which actually looks much better now from a distance); an interesting Revenge figure in *The Spanish Tragedy* (its re-run brilliantly scheduled to play twelve performances in flaming July); an *Uncle Vanya* of which I had high hopes but which crashed on the first night – although I got an Olivier nomination for it; *You Can't Take It With You* – funny previews, unfunny critics. Something in the building was stifling me. I was seeking desperately a way of rebuilding my energy and enthusiasm and challenging myself to break with the repertoire system. Peter Hall posited a series of new companies. I put forward an idea for a touring unit. It would initiate projects outside the building – co-productions – tour them, bring them into The National. A link with the country, an attempt to make The National truly national. I would have my own Administrator, Production Unit, Stage Management team. The grant to The National Theatre that year was some 8% below inflation. The NT was short £1 million. Peter closed The Cottesloe Theatre. My plans went up in smoke. I was VERY grumpy.

I was also burning with anger at the iniquity of the British electoral system. Eleven million people had voted for Thatcher, fourteen million against. Scotland, Wales and the North were almost totally Labour and only in the fat, green, get-rich-quick Yuppie haven of the South did the Conservative Party hold sway. Moreover, Margaret Thatcher had rallied her troops around her with a senseless war of expediency, sailing twelve thousand miles to the Falklands to do battle for 'a little patch of ground that hath in it no profit but the name/To pay five ducats, five, I would not farm it', (*Hamlet*).

The Grand Mechanism of the Polish critic, Jan Kott in *Shakespeare Our Contemporary* was in full sway, the escalator shuttling mice and men up to the top, where the golden crock of Imperialism shone brightly, waiting for the next attempt to snatch it from its podium. Victorian values, under the guise of initiative and incentive, masked the true goal of greed, avarice, exploitation and self. Westminster Rule. Centralisation. Censorship. Power to the City. Bleed the rest of the country dry. Boadicea was in the saddle. The 'rotten parchment bonds' of the fourteenth century were being drawn up again as Britain went into hock, selling herself to any and all who had the money to buy a stake in her and fill the coffers of the fortunate few.

> **This land . . .**
> **Is now leased out . . .**
> **Like to a tenement or pelting farm:**
> **That England, that was wont to conquer others,**
> **Hath made a shameful conquest of itself.**
> **(*Richard II*, II.1)**

Carta Mandua, Queen of the Brigantes, did a deal with the Romans while they were sorting out the Welsh. Sold her country for three hundred and fifty years for a few pieces of plate. Maybe the desire to plunder this few hundred square miles of rock and fields runs deep in the psyche of all those who hold power in their hands. (Then again, Marcos, Ceausescu, Noriega, Milosovitch, Mugabe, Hussein all testify that the latter half of the last century hasn't gone down as the greatest example of universal love.) What price humanity, compassion, equality and freedom? Doors were slammed firmly shut on the sixties. The media were belaboured with a censorship stick.

A conspiracy of silence and complicity surrounded shuffles, resignations, rise and fall, crash and takeover – the desperate feeling of manipulation and manoeuvre in the air. One's life controlled by secret forces and the watching eye. Boardrooms may have replaced the Palace at Westminster, Chairpersons (mainly men) replaced monarchs, but the rules were the same. So what has changed 20 years later I hear you cry?

So. Armed with £100,000 from the Arts Council of Great Britain, similar amounts from the Allied Irish Bank and Canadian philanthropists, Ed and David Mervish, off we trotted to form the English Shakespeare

Company and tackle The Henrys. The parallels were plain. Shakespeare's *Henrys* were plays for today; the Irish problem still with us (still); the Scots clamouring for devolution and the desire to assert their own distinctive culture; the Welsh beleaguered in their welcoming hillsides, fighting a rearguard action to save their language, a million people speaking Welsh; the North laid waste by speculative bulldozers and lack of investment; urban decay hastened by the plethora of concrete car parks and high-rise, high-rent office blocks. Nothing had changed in six hundred years, save the means.

From the moment when an *Ur*-production of *Romeo and Juliet*, set in Renaissance Verona, went down the tubes in Leicester in 1976, my work with Shakespeare had been exclusively modern dress.[1] Each production was successively an attempt to relate and clarify the language and open the plays out for new, young audiences. It was the working out of years of bafflement and frustration as I wrestled desperately with my own incomprehension when presented with obscure, effete, literary productions hailed by the critics as 'masterly re-evaluations'.

However, it was clear to me that total modern dress for *The Henrys* was out. Obvious to anyone, you might say. 'Not so my Lord.' There was no way round the fifth act in *Henry IV Part 1* – the battle scenes and the fight between Hal and Hotspur. Arm wrestling would not do, knives were too mini, a chess match inactive, and omitting it in favour of a newspaper report out of the question. There had to be a final, proper confrontation. After ten years of working exclusively in modern dress, I was about to break the stranglehold it had on me.

The last time I faced the problem was in a previous *Richard III* at The Young Vic Theatre in London in 1979. I cut the fight between Richard and Richmond, substituting a metaphor of Richmond (the butcher) splitting open a real pig's head (representing Richard the Boar) with an axe. Rather good, I thought (until the bills started coming in for dry cleaning from a blood-spattered front row). I couldn't quite bring myself to cut the most famous line in the play (the one about the horse) which was relayed inaudibly from off stage. Milton Shulman, critic of the Evening Standard, in one of his wittier moments, wrote, 'in this production, the least said about Richard's mode of transport, the better.'

So – Elizabethan? Medieval? An option. I was put off, however, by the memory of Trevor Nunn's attempt on Henry IV Part 1 for the opening of The Barbican (the first night impression dominated by the sight of Gerard Murphy as Hal, his armour accidentally reversed on his arms, elbows on the inside, flailing like a demented windmill). Trevor appeared to have submerged both story and politics in an emblematic depiction of medieval pageantry and protocol. The plays seemed hollow.

The Henrys cut a huge swathe across the path of English life at the beginning of the fifteenth century. Yet, of course, the plays are also Elizabethan. Shakespeare analysed the political and social quick-sands of his own time, reflecting what he saw as iniquitous and scurrilous in the make up of the contemporary *moeurs* and *mores* in the mirror of centuries earlier. Or in the mythical lands of Illyria. Or shifting the ground to Athens, Rome, Verona – he was a wily old bird – there was too much at stake to get himself locked up like some of his contemporaries. In a perceptive book, *Political Shakespeare*, edited by Jonathan Dollimore and Alan Sinfield, the contributors analyse the underlying radical political subversion contained in Shakespeare's work, a subversion that is important to hold in mind, for example, in attempting to scrape off the cloying mud of Olivier's propaganda *Henry V*, a film that involved drastic cutting in order to make the jingoistic cap fit.

For some reason I had stick and cloth in my head. I was seeing some combination of tunic, greensward and canvas. Tents, drapes, poles, carpets, curtains. It was a throw-back to an early production of *Sir Gawain and the Green Knight* at the Newcastle Playhouse in 1971. Chris Dyer, the designer, drew some sketches; a combination of the medieval and the modern. Those quick sketches for The Boar's Head Tavern, Glendower's Castle, the Rebel Camp, actually formed the basis for the final production, The Boar's Head looking uncannily like the drawing, even though the stick and cloth idea was soon abandoned. The obvious was staring us in the face, but we had, or I had, avoided facing up to it.

There is a school of thought that believes Shakespeare should be performed in traditional dress and as Shakespeare 'intended'. Oh yes? What *did* Shakespeare intend? Who knows? Nobody and everybody. It is sometimes hard enough with a living author sitting by your side to know what she/he intends. Many a discussion, argument, alteration to a new play is the result of the spoken word often conveying a different meaning from the intention of the written word. I once heard Harold Pinter shouted down at a university drama festival in Bristol because the students did not believe that Pinter understood his own play. It could be. Writing is a mysterious force. The interpretation of combinations of words is an industry in itself. And, of course, finally the responsibility is taken out of the writers' and directors' hands. Actors can change the meaning of a line, a scene, a play, merely with an inflection. The old drama school exercise of a number of ways to say 'To be or not to be'. Interpretation. 'What Shakespeare really meant was . . . ' Who knows? Thank goodness interpretation is subjective. In the final analysis, a combination of words speaks to one person, in one way only. One only has to read widely differing accounts of an actor's performance on the same evening to know that this is a truism. With Shakespeare, due to the volume of received opinion, we are prejudiced before we begin. Nevertheless, there are, in any story, a set of objective circumstances, linked to time and place, that are constant no matter when that story is told. Characters exist in a social and political environment. What gives them their interest is *how* and *why* they relate to each other, given this set of objective circumstances.

The traditional-dress school of thought does not take into consideration that Shakespeare himself often performed the plays in modern dress. Thomas Platter noted in 1599: 'It is the English usage for eminent Lords or Knights at their decease to bequeath and leave almost the best of their clothes to their serving men, which it is unseemly for the latter to wear, so that they offer them then for sale for a small sum to the actors.' A handful of props, a cloak, a crown. When a specific costume is called for, it is usually mentioned in a list of special requirements. That *Julius Caesar* was played completely in togas or *A Midsummer Night's Dream* in short skirts is inconceivable. Soldiers' uniforms were worn with little concern for historical accuracy, if Henry Peacham's drawing of a scene from *Titus Andronicus*, made in about 1595, is any indication. In the drawing the leading character is in some form of Roman dress approximating a toga, while the men flanking him are clearly dressed as Elizabethan soldiers, doublet, hose, pikes and all. 'Traditional dress' is already a nonsense, because in so saying, we certainly do not mean uniformly Elizabethan costume for those plays. True, the Histories would have involved, two hundred years after the event, armour, heraldic surplices, etc, but almost certainly Elizabethan, not authentic medieval, ware.

It was this eclectic theatre of expediency as practised by the Elizabethans that provided the first clue as to how to set, first, *The Henrys* and then continue the style with *The Wars of the Roses*. We would provide a space that would allow the plays to range over the centuries in imagery. We would free our, and the audience's, imaginations by allowing an eclectic mix of costumes and props, choosing a time and a place that was most appropriate for a character or a scene. Modern dress at one moment, medieval, Victorian or Elizabethan the next. We would use a kit of props – chairs, tables, a trolley (we thumbed endless catalogues), a ladder, ammunition boxes, kit bags, a collection of large canvas cloths, suitcases, etc, and we would use them in all combinations possible. The kit, as far as was practicable, would remain on stage. The means of transformation from one scene to the next would remain visible. No tricks up our sleeves (until needed). We would create a style that was essentially rough theatre, but would add, where necessary, a degree of sophistication. It was stick and cloth brought up to date. A stick is a stick, is a stick, until it is a flute, a paddle, a pneumatic drill, a bow and arrow. A trolley is a trolley, until it is a cart, a Land Rover, a carriage. How many ways can you use a British Rail trolley? . . . Answers, please on a postcard to . . . In all this, I should add that there was a degree of expediency – the whole budget for props and furniture was only £10,000. This figure loomed large (or small) in all our discussions.

The setting, we decided, should also reflect the raw approach. We would create a steel structure that would provide a theatre within a theatre, the audience able to see the mechanics of flying, the lighting bridge, the iron-clad framework of the walls of a stage. The bridge should be able to go up and down and operate at several levels. Two sections of the framework should be moveable towers to provide upper levels. In those days we dreamed of fights and chases up and down the towers. We would hang curtains on the struts, and provide a colourful framework for The Boar's Head. The structure and the floor were black. We added a white border to the floor and a back projection screen with a door to the back. The slatted motif of the back projection framework had the feel of a Tudor rose, and the screen had a large, sliding, centre entrance. We added pulleys and ropes to haul canvases up and down. We thought then that the productions would be self-contained, with our own lighting, sound and flying systems, and could therefore play in unconventional spaces

Henry IV, Parts 1 and *2* were looking good, but there was something not working for us in *Henry V*. The eclecticism made us uneasy. Our ingrained modernity was asserting itself. *Henry V*, with its war of expediency, ruthless manipulation, bribery and corruption, palpable pacifism, the French superior in numbers but beaten by superior technology, felt modern. It should be modern.

In his review at The Old Vic the following spring, Guardian critic Michael Billington, tilting with Tillyard, wrote: 'I find Bogdanov's interpretation of England's National Epic wilful, vain and historically dubious. I take Shakespeare's three plays to be complex, ambiguous works about the education of a king; about Hal's immersion in the life of his country in order to become an ideal governor . . . Mr Bogdanov often seems to be overlaying Shakespeare with a play of his own invention . . . *Henry V* also looks forward to the Tudor world in proving that kingliness can be achieved . . . dynastic succession vindicated . . . But my real objection is to the bias that constantly emphasises Hal's ruthlessness at the expense of his humanity.' Billington must have been thinking of another Henry. Kissinger perhaps?

I had looked again, as part of my preparation, at the masterly Orson Welles portrayal of Falstaff in *Chimes at Midnight* (Norman Rodway as Hotspur in a bath tub. An idea I half pinched, setting the same scene with Hotspur shaving). I think the version one of the best Shakespeare films made. Welles edits the two parts of *Henry IV* together, takes some of the dialogue and ideas from *Henry V*, then reshuffles text and story to come up with some extraordinary insights into the character. The film smells of sweat, dirt and war in a way I was never able to capture on stage. I started on too jokey a level with Falstaff's recruiting scene in *Henry IV, Part 2*, for example, and was never able to pull it back. One Wellesian link in particular I seized on. Welles reverses the two parts of the last scene of *Henry IV, Part 1* to leave Hal still at odds with his father. The king patently believes Falstaff has killed Hotspur and that

Hal's claim to have done so is a lie. Obvious. And brilliant. Shakespeare finishes with an apparent reconciliation between father and son at the end of *Part 1*. But then, at the beginning of *Part 2*, they are estranged again, although it is only shortly after the Battle of Shrewsbury. The problem is that he wrote the second part some time after the first. It is possible, though unlikely, that, (a), on completing *Part 1* he didn't know he would write *Part 2* and, (b), taking *Part 1* complete in itself the story had to have a resolution. For us, *Part 2* following *Part 1* on Saturdays one hour later, the effect of finishing Part 1 with the reversal was electric. It left the story wide open, with the audience buzzing with excitement to know what followed. It involved no text alterations. Many a member of the audience came back in the afternoon to find out how the story resolved itself, and then couldn't resist staying for the evening as well – stories of baby-sitting rows, spouses refusing to leave cars behind, emergency arrangements to get home – or stay the night – filtered back every week. Of course, there were always the silly ones who couldn't bear the reversed ending (they should be so lucky to know the text so well in the first place). Thus John Peter in *The Sunday Times*: apart from finding some of the comic business 'coarse beyond belief' and that I suffer from 'dogged attempts' to be 'contemporary', and that 'this sort of rabble-rousing rubbish distorts and vulgarises Shakespeare's cool tough line on power politics', he concludes that I feel that Shakespeare needs my helping hand: ' . . . he switches round the last two scenes of *Part 1* for the sake of what he fondly imagines is a psychological insight.' And then *The Toronto Star*: 'It's all very interesting but it simply isn't Shakespeare. Just by transposing a couple of scenes, director Michael Bogdanov has turned a brilliantly constructed and unified work of art into something that is completely unsatisfying. He could not have said 'to be continued' more clearly if he had had a couple of pom-pom girls parade a banner across the stage.' *Quod erat demonstrandum*. As the story was indeed continued some seventy-five minutes later, I took this intended criticism as a compliment. Something about Shakespeare always brings out the worst in people. The transposition made total sense. Thank you, Orson.

The final rehearsals for the opening in Plymouth took place at the Headquarters of RAF Mountbatten, in a gigantic disused hangar on the sea front and real helicopters took off and landed during rehearsals of the battle sequences in *Henry V*. The Theatre Royal had rigged up our set, lights and sound in this vast, cavernous, corrugated and concrete space, where we had to prepare technically and dress-rehearse the three shows prior to opening cold, with virtually no time on stage, on a Monday night. In the parlous state of the Arts now as then, a theatre cannot afford to lose income being 'dark'.

We were in a hangar, on the sea front. The rain lashed, the wind howled, the blow heaters blew, the company performed heroically. Crucial decisions were taken. I decided to start the cycle with all our kit on stage at the beginning of *Henry IV, Part 1*, so that audiences could see how clever we were in using it all. To understand the set up at the beginning, I decided to re-cap the story of *Richard II* in folk ballad form, a traditional and popular way of telling a story, speaking information. The troubadour tradition.

Taking as its title Hal's name for himself when in disguise on the eve of the battle of Agincourt as he wanders through the camp, that little known Elizabethan/Victorian/ contemporary folk ballad 'Harry Le Roy' was unearthed from the dusty back reaches of Michael Pennington's and my imagination, telling the complete story of *Richard II* in four verses.[2] In America the ballad has been the subject of numerous doctorates. We have always refused to divulge our sources.

I alternated all-night sessions on lights with Chris Ellis, lighting designer, with all-night sessions trying to sort out the music. The extracts that I chose were as eclectic as the costumes, sometimes commenting on the action, sometimes complementing it. Schubert, Berg, Mozart, Handel, The Chieftains, Vaughan Williams, Status Quo's *In the Army Now*, No 1 at the time, seemed to fit perfectly the mood at the end of *Henry IV, Part 2*. Elgar, Purcell, Jarre, Bach. Many pieces I chose were used to stir religious and patriotic memories. Functional 'classic' excerpts, *Zadok the Priest*, *Jerusalem*, *Pomp and Circumstance*. Expediency mainly, culled from various collections to hand.

Bits of old curtain and chenille table cloths were cut up to add a splash of colour to The Boar's Head. Skips and skips and skips of costumes, on loan and eventually hired from The National Theatre, were sifted through, tried on, accepted, rejected, as we attempted to fit characters, scene and mood. John Woodvine as Falstaff for the first time in gigantic white pudding padding, more like Michelin Man than

Falstaff. The uniforms didn't work with the kit of bentwood chairs and the collapsible tables. Rough theatre was foundering on the rock of sophistication. Our splash of colour needed a splash of props to go with it. The sandbags leaked. The sliding screen . . . didn't. The white cloths wouldn't billow, pillow, create snowy landscapes. More a case of the Hesperus crossed with a St Moritz thaw. The tank, collapsible, used for the siege of Harfleur, was divided into two parts. At some venues it had to come from two separate entrances because of space. It was a real wobbly old Heath Robinson affair, the framework held together with pins. Michael leapt on it, staggered each time, regained his balance and began 'Once more unto the breach . . . ' with smoke billowing around him, obscuring both face and voice. The tank fell apart on numerous occasions, finally to disappear from the production altogether halfway through the second year, much to my, but nobody elses, regret. I got my own back last year, 2004, in a documentary for BBCTV, *The Welsh in Shakespeare*, where Michael Sheen declaimed the speech from a real helicopter before soaring high over Carreg Cennen.

It was cold, it was wet, it was windy. It was November. It was chaos. The sea-spray and gales lashed against the corrugated sides of the hangar. In no time, the props and costumes were filthy as they lay on the floor. The screens jammed, broke, tore, didn't close, warped. Made of wood, made on the cheap. Costumes and props went AWOL and no let-up in the afternoon or evening. No breaks for anyone from 8 am till midnight. An acrimonious battle was fought amongst us all to get the production ready in time. With the funds exhausted, Michael and I put our hands in our pockets (not for the last time) to the tune of £5,000 apiece to help the production get there. A desperate air of panic set in among the wardrobe staff and Chris Dyer and I were hardly communicating any more as we wrestled with great white canvas cloths that didn't do any of the things I wanted.

And yet somehow we moved to the theatre to open with *Henry IV, Part 1* on Monday night with a full rehearsal of each of the plays behind us. Wednesday was *Henry IV, Part 2*, Friday *Henry V* and then on Saturday — with no chance of a dry run, the plays unprepared technically — all three.

It is extraordinary that those of us who work in theatre never seem able to understand the process of it. I long ago gave up judging productions at an early stage. Too many shows turn round from one performance to the next. 'I wouldn't go and see it if I were you, it runs for four hours.' 'What? Don't be silly. It's two hours and no interval.' Theatre for me, now, is always work in progress. Just get on with it and try and get it better. And yet how many people in the theatre profession leave a theatre after a preview thinking they have seen a definitive version? 'A funny thing happened on the way from Stratford to London', has written a certain *Guardian* critic on many an occasion. Nothing funny has happened at all. A show has merely played some eighty performances since the first night and is a different production.

As the cheers rang out on that Saturday night, we stood on stage and thought – how stupid can you get? The next three years would show us.

Michael and I jointly pasted up a version of the *Henry VIs*, condensing the three parts into two. The plays sprawl and brawl and they are clearly early works. It is conceivable that the three parts were written in the wrong order. They are probably the result of improvisation and have been tampered with, edited, and the best writing is in *Part 2*. We called our two parts *House of Lancaster* and *House of York*, the first being dominated by the former, the second featuring the rise of the latter. We decided to wrap up the rather rambling Joan of Arc story in the first half of *Lancaster*. It is clear that the original story is weighed down with a fair amount of sixteenth-century English patriotic propaganda, Shakespeare's or otherwise, and we took a crucial decision here to balance the English belief in her as a witch with the French (and her own) as a divinely inspired saviour.

The second half of *Lancaster* would begin with Henry meeting Margaret for the first time and would finish at the death of Suffolk, (Act IV, Scene 1 of Shakespeare's *Part 2*). *House of York* would begin with the Duke of York's return from Ireland and the Jack Cade Rebellion; we would condense the battles and finish the first half of this play with the famous 'Son who killed his father, father who killed his son' scene. The second half would see the rise of Richard Duke of Gloucester leading to his accession as Richard III in the play to follow. We wrote linking lines and passages where necessary to clarify the story and straighten up the loose ends (of which there were many). This became known as 'Bogspeare' although I probably provided only about two thirds of the four hundred-odd lines that were re-written.

It is worth noting that the Peter Hall-John Barton *Wars of the Roses* for The Royal Shakespeare Company included some 1,500 new lines, so we were quite modest really. Our work included such gems as:

KING EDWARD IV: We'll drive the quondam queen into the sea, And make her swim the long way back to France.

and:

SUFFOLK: Fret not yourself my Lord for such reverse.

SOMERSET: Fear you not that, I will not brook this sneap.

and:

WARWICK: Let Richard be restored to his blood, So shall his father's wrongs be recompensed.

SOMERSET: His father was a foul ignoble traitor. Shall he reap honour from his father's shame?

The question of adapting the design style was now vexing us. The rear screen was rebuilt (to work, this time, we hoped), and the flying bridge reconstructed to go down to ground level, which up till then it had been unable to do.

We custom-built the scaffold 'zip-up' towers in lightweight steel to make them easier to negotiate (and more stable). Two sets of steps for ground-level access to the bridge were wheeled on from off-stage. And I introduced a white (grey, actually) circle motif to the glazed floor for *York* and *Lancaster*, reduced the lines of mobile sandbags from two to one and, sadness of sadness, lost the tank. We had started eclectically with the costumes and yet there *was* a sort of chronology to be found. Stephanie proposed that we begin *Richard II* in the Regency period, which would then allow us, with the advent of Bolingbroke as King Henry IV, to retain our Victorian frock coats and scarlet tunics for his court. The *Henry VI*s would progress through the Edwardian period, the

First World War, the twenties and thirties, the Second World War, until we arrived at *Richard III* which I wanted modern and technological. This left *Henry V* as something of an anomaly, as we had already used modern dress in the original production. Accordingly, the suits were replaced with late Victorian frock-coats. The political arena of the plays thus spanned a period of roughly one hundred and fifty years. Street life, battles, etc, retained their eclecticism, though *Henry IV, Parts 1* and *2* remained the best examples of this. I concluded the *Roses* cycle with a conceptual stylistic juxtaposition: switching from modern battle fatigues, the fight between Richmond and Richard III took place in full medieval armour and with long-swords. Two dinosaurs battling for possession. This was followed immediately by Richmond's address to the nation in pin-stripe suit from a TV studio (living proof that there is no quick change in the world that cannot be achieved in thirty seconds). The cycle thus spanned 600 years stylistically. From the point where territorial aggression is resolved by a one-to-one combat for the ruling of a country, to where it is currently at – the media recording events live as they occur in the Balkans, Afghanistan, Iraq.

The Regency style, Beau Brummell dandyism, suited our purposes; a profligate, dilettante Richard II. I suspect that were I to embark on a one-off production of the play this is not the period I would ideally choose – don't ask me which – I don't know, never having thought about it any other way. Michael and I decided that we wanted Richard surrounded by music and artists, a contrast to the puritan austerity of Bolingbroke Rule. The 1960s to 1980s? It would be colourful before turning dark and Victorian. Attempting a setting for this sumptuous scenario within the framework of our steely black structure was a poser; I added three sets of net curtains – all we could afford – sprayed the back set purple and left the two front sets white. We 'rouched' them. This allowed for a certain amount of softness when properly arranged, but did not quite match the velveteened volumes of the imagination, great swathes of silk and satin festooned liberally in the great hall surrounded by gilded oils and Louis Quinze. What we *did* have was our (my) bits of chenille tablecloth that we had used to dress the tavern in the Boar's Head. They would have to do. I draped the throne (symbol of misuse), an easel, the card table, three chairs and a cushion. Later we bought a few off-cuts of velvet. It did. Just.

Our versions of the *Henry VI*s were greeted with enthusiasm although the originals were soon brought out as the company culled stricken couplets from their folders with, 'There's a couple of lines here that you've left out and I'm not sure why . . . ' The deal was – anything could be re-inserted provided an actor was prepared to lose the same amount in exchange. To be fair, most of the company adhered to this side of the bargain. Although there were themes to follow as in *The Henrys*, it was naturally far harder to rehearse seven plays all at once and to keep the strands in one's head, and *House of Lancaster* and *House of York* were, in effect, two new texts started from scratch.

The *Henry VI* rehearsals were fast and furious. Discuss a scene, improvise it, set it. If satisfied, send it away with Assistant Directors Stella Bond and Sue Best to be worked on. And so many fights. There is always a problem with suspension of disbelief in staging medieval fights involving large numbers. Mostly, elephantine cavorting in suits of armour, wielding balls and chains and swords too heavy to lift, makes me laugh. In this frame of mind I had no wish to be hoist by my own petard.

Finally, I condensed all the big battles into ones of single combat, the sole remaining large one, known as 'the *York* rumble', finding its way into performance before being cut on our return from Australia, in late autumn 1988. However, there was still quite a lot of running on and off stage and obligatory smoke.

The choices of music were mainly from earlier periods with a few exceptions. Harsh, atonal bars from Berg's Violin Concerto introduced the rose-picking Temple Garden scene in the *House of Lancaster*, an indication of future disintegration; a jagged electronic theme from an unknown horror movie helped decapitate Suffolk. Henry VI's piety was emphasised by the use of a solo choir boy singing Psalm 121: 'I will lift up mine eyes unto the Lord'; a Gregorian chant accompanied Henry V's funeral and the deaths of Mortimer, Lancaster and Beaufort. All the battle scenes echoed to cannon fire and Byrd's *Mass for Four Voices*, emphasising the religious justification voiced by the participants. Live accordion music for the French victory at Orleans, and Henry VI's Coronation in France was introduced with Mozart's *Coronation Mass*. His wedding to Margaret was celebrated with Handel's *Music for the Royal Fireworks*. Various other court scenes in England were accompanied by Monteverdi's *Vespers* and Pergolesi's *Stabat Mater*. The same themes were used yet again in House of York but became more modern with *Glassworks* by Philip Glass and Louis Armstrong's *Alligator Crawl* which was used as background for Edward IV's Cocktail Party, beginning the second half. The long-sword/armour fight between Richmond and Richard was fought out to the strains of Samuel Barber's *Adagio for Strings*. It was a trick picked up from the film *Platoon*. Yes, Michael Coveney, Samuel Barber, *not* Mahler's Eighth.[3]

Believing in the divinity of Joan of Arc was proving a problem, and Mary Rutherford and I worked on the mysterious ethereal aspect; difficult, given the lack of text to do it with. I don't think I helped by loading down her supernatural powers with Peruvian pipes reminiscent of the film *Picnic at Hanging Rock*.

Louis Potter later wrote in *The Times Literary Supplement* (in a review otherwise extremely complimentary): 'The one failure to confront the text is the treatment of Joan of Arc . . . No devils appear to her. La Pucelle is played as the dazed recipient of an incomprehensible magic; the music that accompanies her throughout her success suggests fairy land, and when it abandons her, the effect is of a performance of *Peter Pan* where no one claps in order to save Tinkerbell.' It *was* kitsch, though liked by many.

In fact I was struggling altogether to find depth in *House of Lancaster*. The downfall of Gloucester hinges on witchcraft. His wife dabbles in the occult in an attempt to find out whether her husband will be king or not. The predictions of the medium come true, in point of fact. The trap is to burden this scene down with a lot of comic mumbo jumbo. I fell right in. As with the Gads Hill fight in *Henry IV, Part 1* and the Recruiting Scene in *Henry IV, Part 2*, so far in that it was difficult to pull the scene back. The séance table won the Naff Prop prize for the tour. An empty goblet was to spill and run blood, a knife was to up end itself suddenly and sink into the table, an empty glass to fill with water. Passing through the surface was a network of tubes, wires and strings, leading to squeezy bottles . . . . Derek Scriminger, Stage Manager, the tallest of tall, for some reason elected to crouch under the table and work it all and succeeded only in soaking himself with water and diluted ketchup. Ditto the stage crew – our attempt at ectoplasm resulted in Barry Stanton as Bolingbroke the Conjurer winding his head and arms in white bandage like some Frankenstein emerging from his operation. The thunder and lightning emphasised the silliness of it all. Impossible after all this to take seriously the Hawking Scene that follows, where a blind man has to have his sight restored and then recovers the use of his leg by another 'miracle'. The problem with rehearsing such scenes so fast is that it leads to easy options, humour being the road of least resistance. It is easier to invent comic business quickly and leave the actors to develop it on their own, than to painstakingly (and painfully) build up the truth and reality of such skimpily written situations. Nevertheless, when so much 'real' action depends on the consequences, time must be taken. I didn't, and the result was always an uphill struggle to make the plot hang together in the second half of *House of Lancaster*. That we did, on occasions, succeed, given no time to re-conceive or re-rehearse, is a testimony to the actors' belief that they had to sacrifice the laughs in the service of the story.

Another road of least resistance, I suppose, was the developing of the hooligan, National Front theme in *House of York* in the form of the Cade Rebellion. Could one believe that this drink-sodden, totem-twirling, Union Jack brigade of Doc Martened bovver boys could ever take over the running of the country?

Michael Pennington turned Jack Cade into a machete-twirling tornado, with spiky red hair and a Union Jack vest. The chant of 'you're gonna get your fuckin' heads kicked in' rang out weekly on stage as pitched battles raged on sea ferries to the same cries and the Heysel Stadium collapsed. Europe certainly doesn't believe such groups could never take over the country.

In week six, tragedy struck. On Saturday afternoon I had been rehearsing with John Price. He had a fight call with Malcolm and Ian Burford on the York-Clifford duel in *House of York* and then we proceeded to have a marvellous Bolingbroke rehearsal. We also worked on an idea for a Dave Allen-style introduction to the whole cycle. Before the beginning of *Richard II*, we would set a table, a glass, John sitting there casually, a cigarette, lights down, then: 'Edward III, my Lord, had seven sons – are you with me so far?' and then he would go through the whole rigmarole of the royal succession, taken from the second part of *Henry VI*. John was in great form. We laughed and joked and finished at six o'clock with John enthusing about the idea and taking it away to develop it.

I was never to find out if it was a good idea or not. The following day I had a call to say that John had slipped and fallen while in the bathroom, had knocked himself unconscious and was in hospital. The next day was to reveal that in fact John had suffered a stroke. At that stage there was no cause for alarm but, as the days passed and John showed no signs of recovering consciousness, the awful truth of the situation began to dawn on us. When the news came that the doctors had switched off John's life support system, the tears flowed unrestrainedly. He had come into my life as an actor only one year before. We had fought, argued, discussed, laughed and enthused together and had become the firmest of friends professionally and personally. He was like a wolf – lean, lank, dark, gangling. But friendly, benign, his soft brown eyes quizzical, questioning. Hal's Angel.

With a critically short rehearsal period, we were now in deep trouble. John Castle, with whom I had coincided at Trinity College, Dublin, agreed to take over the roles of Bolingbroke, Pistol and York. It would take him all his time to learn the words. How would I ever be able to fill in any detail for him? We both agreed that I was to carry on with my normal schedule and he would catch up as best he could.

The last week in November. We moved into our end phase, for technical rehearsals. This time, it was to what was laughingly called a 'studio' in Limehouse. It was an old storage warehouse, barely large enough, measuring some fifty foot by seventy. One end had a huge entrance, obviously for container lorries, and no doors. It would have to be blocked up. So would the holes in the roof, the holes in the walls. It had been the mildest of autumns but, as luck would have it, the weather turned nasty for the two weeks that we were there. Rain, wind, snow, sleet, we had everything the Thames, ten yards away, could throw at us. We had underestimated and under-budgeted the extras.

At that level, production management in London is a Mafia activity. Call in all sorts of favours, do deals, trade in one small job on one production against a big one on another. Grease palms, scratch backs, turn blind eyes, etc. Sometimes it's a very close wind-sailing job. Simon Opie was a master mediator.

True, we *did* overspend. Michael and I dipped into our pockets yet again. This time it was to supply the armour and video camera for the end of *Richard III*. As I had pointed out to Prue Skene, Administrator, there wasn't anything else in *Richard III*. Just modern suits. The armour and video were the only real props and without them the production – indeed the whole cycle – had no climax.

And the same scramble on costumes as the year before.

We froze on. Coughs and colds notwithstanding, we managed to get some sort of a run of all seven plays. There was an awful lot to do in Bath. The pattern for the openings was –

Tuesday 8th December: *Richard II*
Wednesday 9th: *Henry IV, Part 1*
Thursday 10th: *Henry IV, Part 2*
Friday 11th: *Henry V*
Saturday 12th: *Richard II and Henry IV, Parts 1 and 2*
Monday 14th: *Henry VI, House of Lancaster*
Tuesday 15th: *Henry VI, House of York*
Wednesday 16th: *Richard III*

I don't suppose we can claim a world record, but opening seven shows, twenty four hours of Shakespeare in nine days is not bad going. Don't boast, don't complain. Why bother? What's the point? What are you trying to prove? A familiar argument ran: 'If the circumstances are so rushed, and the compromise so great, what's the point of it all? Why fuck up a great set of plays just to show you can get them on? Anyone can do shoddy, ill-prepared, technically unsound work.' It *was* an achievement just to get them on. But the reasons for doing it ran much deeper. Despite all the obvious drawbacks, there was paradoxically one great advantage.

Artistic freedom. Even if the compromises at times seemed unending, in another way the line was straight and true. The release of the language, the quality of the story-telling, at its best, was exhilarating. Nobody can get a production right. As a director, you do one good one, one bad one, one medium. You spend your time trying to eliminate the bad one. Then with one good and two medium, you're pretty good. With two good and one medium, you're world class. And here we were with seven on offer. It's a very simple equation really. If you get 90% of a production right (what is right?) you are a world beater. At 75% it is a great production and about the most that any self-respecting director can hope for. The problem with getting even 75% of *The Wars of the Roses* right, however, is that while out of twenty four hours eighteen might be passable, that still leaves six whole hours that are naff! That's two whole plays! Which two? I hear you cry. Opinions vary. And if Bath Theatre Royal was too small the year before, this time it was pretty catastrophic. We knew the routine, however. Build a platform out the back for the lights, to store the props, etc. The weather in December that year was mercifully mild, no repeat of the previous year's audience deep freeze. For some unfathomable reason, known only to the gods of theatre statistics, the year before, the turnover had been sensational. This time the public, if not exactly staying away, were not exactly besieging the box office either. From being one of the most successful venues, Bath turned out to be almost our worst. Why? It was the same time of year, the weather better, four new plays on offer. Was it an omen? *Richard II*, the first one in, was certainly pretty shaky. Very long, the first performance, three and a half hours – amazing the number of people who, having seen that opening night, were to say two years later, 'Funny, it's changed beyond all recognition.'

Really none of the shows was up to much, and *House of York* and *Lancaster* were very messy. Each of them contained twenty four fast-moving scenes. They needed tightening. The best was *Richard III*. It was clear that Andy was going to deliver all that he had promised in rehearsal, and the two scenes at the end were sensational. Andy's armour only just arrived in time for the Bath opening, and when he donned it we discovered to our horror that the hump had been built on the wrong side of his back. In a series of frantic phone calls, we ascertained that there was just enough time to get it changed. Straps and buckles were to break, and bits fly off – one of the penalties of tight budgets. The 'quick changes' in and out of costume on that first performance took an eternity. *Richard III* ran four hours. I had written *à la* Jan Kott a staged introduction to the central characters. The company was split as to its necessity, and to the end opinion was divided. I thought that maybe it was necessary for single performances, but for trilogies and cycles . . . Barry Stanton had not had time to learn it and carried a folder as if he were a 'Miss World/Come Dancing' compère.

This Introduction, effected in elegant thirties cream outfits to the background of a cool modern jazz number played by the company, went down sensationally. Not that the laughter was all intentional. As when John Darrell stepped forward, bass guitar strapped to his white suit, to be announced as Earl Rivers . . . 'And there you have it, the Woodvilles, the Plantagenets, the Politicians, the Ladies.'

We filmed the whole cycle in the very last week of our three year marathon at the Grand Theatre Swansea. Live. One a night. With eight cameras and a camera team who had never seen the shows before…The Wars of the Roses – the Nightmare Continues. The videos (now available on DVD) are, as you would expect, rough. They do, however, despite the blemishes and tired, uneven performances, give some idea of the extraordinary achievement of a company that dared.

These essays are an attempt to give some further insight into the thinking behind those productions and why collectively the Histories form such a monumental part of our dramatic heritage, painting as they do an incisive picture of our nation, the colours as vivid today as four or six hundred years ago.

If there are a few too many references to the Iraq war – *tant pis*. As Brecht said, the theatre should always be mindful of the needs of its time and our time, and has been dominated by the consequences of that Bush/Blair folly. I have always believed that theatre should have both an umbilical cord to the street and reflect the day's headlines. Were I to direct the Wars of the Roses today . . .

Michael Bogdanov, April 2005[4]

Notes

1. See *Shakespeare - The Director's Cut, Volume 1*.

2. See Appendix II.

3. *Financial Times*, 21st January 1989.

4. This Introduction is adapted from *The English Shakespeare Company, The Story of 'The Wars of the Roses' 1986-1989* by Michael Bogdanov and Michael Pennington, Nick Hern Books, 1989, (www.nickhernbooks.co.uk).

Richard II

The skipping King

Richard II is the only Shakespeare play that is written entirely in verse and in a good deal of rhyming couplets at that. There is an almost relentless hammering of what in any other playwright would be doggerel. Yet the play manages to be one of his most lyrical and despite what seems to be a constraint of style, the writing is positively elegiac.

The figure of Richard himself starts on an almost superficial level, his casual way of ruling alienating the audience and focusing attention and sympathy on his victims. Yet as the play progresses, Shakespeare manages to turn the tide and as our compassion for this wayward, selfish king grows, so does our mistrust of Bolingbroke and his cronies. As with many of Shakespeare's protagonists, we lament the passing of colour and greet the era of conformity with suspicion.

The problem of pre-history in Richard II is immediately apparent in the very first scene that opens the play. In fact, the whole History cycle is a Pandora's box of onions that peel away, *Peer Gynt*-like, to nothing. The subject is the murder of the Duke of Gloucester, Thomas of Woodstock which has taken place before the play starts.

Bolingbroke accuses Mowbray of being responsible of Woodstock's death, thereby indirectly accusing Richard, on whose orders Mowbray was acting, thus sparking off a challenge to a duel. Mowbray covers up for Richard – *this time*.

What does Richard do? If Bolingbroke wins, as is likely, he becomes all powerful, proved right. His next tilt could be at the King himself – in fact, it is. He has to go.

In the unlikely event of Mowbray winning, he has a strong hold over Richard. He *definitely* has to go – for ever. You cannot have a courtier hanging around with grounds for blackmail, though Mowbray has grounds to be miffed inasmuch as he gets life, whereas Bolingbroke, the initiator of the challenge, only gets seven years.

A miscalculation on Richard's part – the first of many. The duel is not the answer, and Richard knows it. He can't risk a winner. But he plays the game. Why? Probably just enjoys the thrill of power. Ever the actor, he lets the duel go ahead, with ritual, pomp and pageantry, all the way right up to the moment of truth when, with a theatrical flourish, he stops the action.

> **LORD MARSHAL: Sound, trumpets; and set forward, combatants!**
> *A charge sounded. King Richard throws his warder into the lists*
> **Stay! The King hath thrown his warder down.**
>
> **KING RICHARD: Let them lay by their helmets and their spears**
> **And both return back to their chairs again.**
> *(To his counsellors)*
> **Withdraw with us, and let the trumpets sound**
> **While we return these dukes what we decree.**
> **(Act I.3)**

Our understanding of all this hinges therefore on our recognition of what lies behind Bolingbroke's challenge to Mowbray, and what appears to be Richard's whim in prematurely interrupting the duel.

How to make all this clear? Even an old play, *Thomas of Woodstock* (anonymous), dealing with the murder, isn't much help, focusing as it does on the deed without implicating Richard. There's nothing really for a director to lift that would make the situation more accessible and I suspect the answer lies in creating a pre-scene showing the murder and those involved, as one would do on film. Olivier, in both *Henry V* and *Richard III*, created pre-scenes explaining past events.

In the second scene, the Duchess of Gloucester, Thomas of Woodstock's widow, pleads with John of Gaunt, Woodstock's brother, to do something about her husband's murder. John of Gaunt refuses.

> **JOHN OF GAUNT: God's is the quarrel; for God's substitute,**
> **His deputy anointed in His sight,**
> **Hath caused his death; the which if wrongfully,**
> **Let heaven revenge, for I may never lift**

An angry arm against His minister.

Clear as daylight. As long as you know that he's talking about Richard. The language is complex, the references oblique. Neither the Duchess nor John of Gaunt ever mentions Richard by name, yet knowledge of the king's participation in the crime is crucial to our understanding of why Richard has to get rid of both Mowbray and Bolingbroke. He doesn't effectively do either for exiling Bolingbroke was no solution; back he comes, a usurper, grabs the throne and does for Richard.

For this is where it all begins. The Wars of the Roses. A hundred years of dynastical slaughter and mayhem because, for those who believe in it, the order of history has been disturbed:

KING RICHARD: . . . Not all the water in the rough rude sea
Can wash the balm from an anointed king.
The breath of worldly men cannot depose
The deputy elected by the Lord.
(Act III.2)

There is a natural order to the universe; everything has its place, and divine right is part of that order. Provided, of course, that it's a Tudor king. (Don't question too closely who first decreed that – you might come up with the right answer).

As proof of Shakespeare's belief in the status quo, conservatives are often wont to quote, completely out of context, Ulysses' speech from *Troilus and Cressida* outlining this natural order.

O, when degree is shaked,
Which is the ladder to all high designs,
The enterprise is sick. How could communities,
Degrees in schools, and brotherhoods in cities,
Peaceful commerce from dividable shores,
The primogenitive and due of birth,
Prerogative of age, crowns, sceptres, laurels,
But by degree, stand in authentic place?
Take but degree away, untune that string,

And hark what discord follows!
(*Troilus and Cressida* **I.3**)

Don't rock the boat, let sleeping dogs lie, anything for an easy life, we've always done it this way so why change? This may do for some, but I'm damned if it did for Shakespeare.

* * *

Shakespeare drew practically all his material for *Richard II* from Rafael Holinshed's *Chronicles of England, Scotland and Ireland*, which was first published in 1577. Probably he used the second edition of 1587, since the portent of the withering of the bay trees in Act II.2 is not recorded in the first. Here, the Welsh captain sees this and other manifestations as omens and, having waited for Richard to arrive from Ireland for over a week, the Welsh soldiers disperse.[1] It is one of those Thomas Hardy-esque ironies that if Richard had arrived a day earlier he would have had the support of an army and Bolingbroke might never have succeeded in imprisoning him in Flint Castle.

> **CAPTAIN: . . . We will not stay.**
> **The bay trees in our country are all withered,**
> **And meteors fright the fixèd stars of heaven.**
> **The pale-faced moon looks bloody on the earth,**
> **And lean-looked prophets whisper fearful change.**
> **Rich men look sad, and ruffians dance and leap –**
> **The one in fear to lose what they enjoy,**
> **The other to enjoy by rage and war.**
> **These signs forerun the death or fall of kings.**
> **Farewell. Our countrymen are gone and fled,**
> **As well assured Richard their king is dead.**
> **(Act II.4)**

Scenes that are not in the original Holinshed are some of the most moving and lyrical in the play: Gaunt and the widowed Duchess of Gloucester; Gaunt's death; the gardeners at York; Richard's abdication; the parting of the deposed king and his queen; the story of the groom

– these are Shakespeare's own, and throughout, a giant unseen presence looms over the play. An inanimate character who nonetheless lives, breathes, expands, contracts, laughs, cries and generally hovers over the action as an anxious guardian angel.

It is England. This England. 'This royal throne of kings'. 'This blessed plot, this earth, this realm' is a fertile garden, a manor house, a fortress. Those who inhabit it only do so courtesy of her grace. The people do not own it, it is loaned to them. But England has a problem. He's called Richard II. He is destroying this England. He is abusing the trust that has been invested in him and England is bleeding to death in his care.

Richard is politically incompetent and unpopular: The Earl of Northumberland accuses him of gross abuse of the public purse and of being 'basely led/By flatterers'; Ross laments the 'grievous taxes' he has levied to pay for the Irish wars and his own wild extravagance; Willoughby complains that 'daily new exactions are devised'. In Richard's desperate search to fill his coffers to maintain his lifestyle, England itself is being auctioned off. Close to death at the start of Act II, John of Gaunt gives voice to the criticism piling up around Richard's head:

> Now he that made me knows I see thee ill;
> Ill in myself to see, and in thee seeing ill.
> Thy deathbed is no lesser than thy land,
> Wherein thou liest in reputation sick;
> And thou, too careless patient as thou art,
> Committest thy anointed body to the cure
> Of those 'physicians' that first wounded thee.
> A thousand flatterers sit within thy crown,
> Whose compass is no bigger than thy head . . .
> Landlord of England art thou now, not king.
> Thy state of law is bondslave to the law,
> And thou –
> (Act II.1)

and Richard, bored, rudely interrupts:

> RICHARD: . . . a lunatic lean-witted fool,
> Presuming on an ague's privilege,

> Darest with thy frozen admonition
> Make pale our cheek, chasing the royal blood
> With fury from his native residence.
> Now by my seat's right royal majesty,
> Wert thou not brother to great Edward's son,
> This tongue that runs so roundly in thy head
> Should run thy head from thy unreverent shoulders.

Shakespeare seems intent on making the man as unlikeable as possible. When he first hears of Gaunt's illness he flippantly remarks,

> Forget, forgive, conclude and be agreed;
> Our doctors say this is no month to bleed.
> (Act I.1)

This deepens into a speech of contemptuous and shocking callousness on the news that Gaunt is close to death:

> Now put it, God, in the physician's mind
> To help him to his grave immediately!
> The lining of his coffers shall make coats
> To deck our soldiers for these Irish wars.
> Come, gentlemen, let's all go visit him.
> Pray God we may make haste and come too late!
> (Act 1.4)

The comparison here is with Richard III, but whereas we are intrigued and amused at the brazen effrontery of Richard III's scurrility, here there is something distasteful and offensive. Now close to death, John of Gaunt gives us his view of an ideal England that is being decimated. With the prescience of a clairvoyant, he prefigures Henry VI when he says:

> Methinks I am a prophet new-inspired,
> And thus, expiring, do foretell of him:
> His rash fierce blaze of riot cannot last;
> For violent fires soon burn out themselves.

Small showers last long, but sudden storms are short.
(Act II.1)

Predicting that the king's vanity will ruin him, he suddenly launches off into a prophesy of England's imminent destruction. John of Gaunt's love of his country stands diametrically opposed to the contemptuous mishandling of its sacred qualities by Richard in God's name.

This royal throne of kings, this sceptred isle,
This earth of majesty, this seat of Mars,
This other Eden – demi-paradise –
This fortress built by Nature for herself
Against infection and the hand of war,
This happy breed of men, this little world,
This precious stone set in the silver sea,
Which serves it in the office of a wall,
Or as a moat defensive to a house
Against the envy of less happier lands;
This blessèd plot, this earth, this realm, this England . . .
(Act 11.1)

Gaunt predicates everything that England should be under Richard's rule but patently isn't. The nation is:

This nurse, this teeming womb of royal kings,
Feared by their breed, and famous by their birth,
Renownèd for their deeds as far from home
For Christian service and true chivalry
As is the sepulchre in stubborn Jewry
Of the world's ransom, blessèd Mary's son;
This land of such dear souls, this dear dear land,
Dear for her reputation through the world,
Is now leased out – I die pronouncing it –
Like to a tenement or pelting farm.
England, bound in with the triumphant sea,
Whose rocky shore beats back the envious siege
Of watery Neptune, is now bound in with shame . . .

That England that was wont to conquer others
Hath made a shameful conquest of itself.
(Act 11.1)

Richard's betrayal of England is compounded by a further demonstration of personal contempt for individual life and feeling. Just moments after Gaunt's death, the king cynically announces that he will seize his 'plate, coin, revenues, and movables' in order to fund the Irish wars – in effect dispossessing Gaunt's banished son, Bolingbroke, of his inheritance and thereby triggering the events that will end in Richard's abdication. Ignoring York's eloquent plea to honour the life of dedication that John of Gaunt has given to his country and the crown, Richard coolly repeats, 'Think what you will: we seize into our hands/His plate, his goods, his money, and his lands.' What has changed? Today, in hock to big business, globalisation, and our 'special' relationship, Britain is once again leased out, a 'landlord' in charge, not a ruler.

Gardens are everywhere in the play, but 'This other Eden' of John of Gaunt's has been over-farmed, transformed from a green, colourful, luxurious and verdant source of nourishment into a barren wasteland of overworked fields, disappearing hedgerows and endangered wildlife. Pesticides have decimated indigenous plants and the soil lies poisoned and polluted. It is badly in need of resuscitation – a great deal of suckling, nurturing and TLC. The gardeners put it succinctly in Act III.4:

GARDENER: *(to one man)*
Go, bind thou up young dangling apricocks
Which, like unruly children, make their sire
Stoop with oppression of their prodigal weight.
Give some supportance to the bending twigs.
(To the other)
Go thou, like an executioner
Cut off the heads of too fast-growing sprays
That look too lofty in our commonwealth.
All must be even in our government.
You thus employed, I will go root away
The noisome weeds which without profit suck

The soil's fertility from wholesome flowers.

FIRST MAN: Why should we, in the compass of a pale,
Keep law and form and due proportion,
Showing as in a model our firm estate,
When our sea-wallèd garden, the whole land,
Is full of weeds, her fairest flowers choked up,
Her fruit trees all unpruned, her hedges ruined,
Her knots disordered, and her wholesome herbs
Swarming with caterpillars?

The gardeners lament the fact that Richard has not tended his garden and reluctantly admit the need for a wholesale clearout of the weeds that are choking the earth. That means getting rid of Richard and chums, and accepting the rule of Bolingbroke. There is a feeling of regret for the passing of such a colourful character. If only Richard had done what they do:

GARDENER: . . . O, what a pity is it
That he had not so trimmed and dressed his land
As we this garden! We at time of year
Do wound the bark, the skin of our fruit trees,
Lest being overproud in sap and blood
With too much riches it confound itself.
Had he done so to great and growing men
They might have lived to bear, and he to taste
Their fruits of duty. Superfluous branches
We lop away that bearing boughs may live.
Had he done so, himself and borne the crown
Which waste of idle hours hath quite thrown down.

The gardeners are at one with John of Gaunt's vision. From both ends of the spectrum the picture of England is one of devastating neglect. A rich, fecund land suffering under the yoke of tyranny. Richard had to go. But why must the pendulum always swing so violently back the other way? Would you want a Bolingbroke to marry your sister?

In fact Richard's reign sounds rather exciting – music and dance, fun and games, lots of stand-up. Arts and sport and plenty of partying. Problem is, he pushed it all a bit too far and when the money ran out . . . well, so did his friends. Shades of Timon of Athens.

> **KING HENRY: . . . The skipping King, he ambled up and down,**
> **With shallow jesters, and rash bavin wits,**
> **Soon kindled and soon burnt, carded his state,**
> **Mingled his royalty with capering fools,**
> **Had his great name profanèd with their scorns,**
> **And gave his countenance against his name**
> **To laugh at gibing boys, and stand the push**
> **Of every beardless vain comparative,**
> **Grew a companion to the common streets,**
> **Enfeoffed himself to popularity,**
> **That, being daily swallowed by men's eyes,**
> **They surfeited with honey, and began**
> **To loathe the taste of sweetness, whereof a little**
> **More than a little is by much too much.**
> **So, when he had occasion to be seen,**
> **He was but as the cuckoo is in June,**
> **Heard, not regarded . . .**
> **(*Henry IV, Part 1*, Act III.2)**

Do we believe this description of Richard from a man who was so patently biased? Who continually convinces himself that tomorrow is the day he'll go on that pilgrimage to the Holy Land? He really will. Our advantage as an audience watching the plays chronologically is that we've already seen Richard II in action and can measure Bolingbroke's view of him against what we have seen. It provides a fascinating duality of choice in the story-telling. To confound or not to confound the audience's expectations.

Bolingbroke naturally fancies himself as the antithesis of all this, his view of himself shot through with the prim Puritanism of an austere recluse. A self-appointed arbiter of public morality: A one-man Viewers and Listeners Association.

> **KING HENRY: . . . Had I so lavish of my presence been,**
> **So common-hackneyed in the eyes of men,**

So stale and cheap to vulgar company,
Opinion, that did help me to the crown,
Had still kept loyal to possession,
And left me in reputeless banishment,
A fellow of no mark nor likelihood.
By being seldom seen, I could not stir
But like a comet I was wondered at,
That men would tell their children, 'This is he!'
Others would say, 'Where, which is Bolingbroke?'
And then I stole all courtesy from heaven,
And dressed myself in such humility
That I did pluck allegiance from men's hearts,
Loud shouts and salutations from their mouths,
Even in the presence of the crownèd King.
Thus did I keep my person fresh and new,
My presence, like a robe pontifical,
Ne'er seen but wondered at, and so my state,
Seldom, but sumptuous, showed like a feast,
And won by rareness such solemnity.
(*Henry IV, Part 1*, Act III.2)

What Bolingbroke neglects to say is that he nicked the crown in the first place. And herein lies the difference in the two regimes. The one artistic, insouciant, profligate – the other devious, austere, philistine. Thatcher after the 60s, suits instead of flares.

Richard II is not merely de-throned, he is hurled into the abyss and with him the structure of the feudal world. The fire of the sun-king is doused, the glass is smashed, the natural order is disturbed, and Richard is no longer a king but a mere mortal. The problem with thinking (and believing) that you are the Lord's anointed is that you end up on the plus side of arrogant. Humility and listening are not qualities synonymous with those who believe themselves untouchable. Not that Richard was a Medieval Bagwan, but the seeds of his downfall are in his contempt for anything that smacks of the democratic process. He has abused and violated his position and, in trying to invoke the divine mystique of kingship, all he is capable of is hollow rhetoric:

> For every man that Bolingbroke hath pressed
> To lift shrewd steel against our golden crown,
> God for his Richard hath in heavenly pay
> A glorious angel. Then if angels fight,
> Weak men must fall; for heaven still guards the right.
> *Enter Salisbury*
> Welcome, my lord. How far off lies your power?
> (Act III.2)

Wonderful. While purporting to believe that his divinity is hedged, his immediate problem is the number of soldiers he's got to protect him. Fantasy and reality collide, with reality the winner. And the reality is that he is a weak, self-indulgent wastrel who hastens his own downfall with a streak of paranoid defeatism. It is easier to wallow in a slough of despond than find the will to act positively in his own defence. It is also more satisfying, more exciting, and in trying to keep control of his own ruin, Richard falls faster than anyone can push him, hastening his own mixed metaphor demise by being one jump ahead:

> RICHARD: What must the king do now?
> . . . Must he lose
> The name of king? A God's name, let it go.
> (Act III.3)

Here lies the principal contrast between the 'skipping king' and the 'vile politician'. Bolingbroke stakes out the territory carefully, moving forward slowly, sweeping the ground for hidden mines, his true purpose, that of taking the crown, veiled until he is absolutely sure of support for his aim. Paradoxically it is Richard who forces the pace and flushes Bolingbroke's real motives out into the open. Richard who finally gets under Bolingbroke's skin, forcing an admission of his true purpose:

> RICHARD: . . . Set on towards London, cousin, is it so?

(ie, the Tower).

BOLINGBROKE: Yea, my good lord.

RICHARD: Then I must not say no.

London, the seat of power, where power changes hands. But Richard is not going to go quietly. Oh, no. The actor in him ensures that he will cause Bolingbroke the maximum embarrassment. He leads him to believe that the hand-over will be easy.

BOLINGBROKE: Fetch hither Richard, that in common view
He may surrender. So we shall proceed
Without suspicion.
(Act IV.1)

Ever cautious, Bolingbroke needs this public display of surrender to avoid the accusation of a behind-doors *putsch*. It's called covering your arse. Richard, however, despite what appeared earlier to be meek compliance, has other ideas. A public platform? Perfect for a consummate drama queen:

RICHARD: . . . To what service am I sent for hither?

Shocked pause. Wait a minute, it wasn't supposed to happen like this. The very office of kingship is degraded by that word 'service'. Chauffeur? Head cook and bottle washer?

BOLINGBROKE: I thought you had been willing to resign.

That's it. The word is out in the open. Richard's cue for a display of theatrical fireworks. The prosaic Bolingbroke can now only be a helpless bystander as the process of handing over the crown becomes an humiliating farce.

RICHARD: Give me the crown.
Here, cousin – seize the crown. Here, cousin –
On this side, my hand; and on that side, thine.
Now is this golden crown like a deep well

> That owes two buckets, filling one another,
> The emptier ever dancing in the air,
> The other down, unseen, and full of water.
> That bucket down and full of tears am I,
> Drinking my griefs whilst you mount up on high.
> (Act IV.1)

Two grown men, the most powerful in the land, like two dogs fighting over a piece of meat clenched between their teeth. Both have their hand on the crown, neither wearing it; a pathetic tug of war, one of the most disturbing moments of Roses history, rivalling Queen Margaret wiping the Duke of York's face with a cloth steeped in the blood of his murdered son in *Henry VI, Part 3*.

Richard suddenly switches his mode of speech, formality replacing his earlier insouciance. He turns the coronation ceremony upside down, contemptuously demonstrating that he knew what the sanctity of kingship really is about all along. He tears up the rule book in a grotesque parody of that ceremony:

> . . . Now, mark me how I will undo myself.
> I give this heavy weight from off my head,
> And this unwieldy sceptre from my hand,
> The pride of kingly sway from out my heart.
> With mine own tears I wash away my balm,
> With mine own hands I give away my crown,
> With mine own tongue deny my sacred state,
> With mine own breath release all duteous oaths.
> All pomp and majesty I do forswear.
> My manors, rents, revenues, I forgo.
> My acts, decrees, and statutes I deny.
> God pardon all oaths that are broke to me;
> God keep all vows unbroken are made to thee;

Richard is the judge, jury and presiding officer at his own downfall, and in a storming finale, creates for himself and the onlookers a mock ritual for the handing-over ceremony, deliberately pointing up the absurdity of the deposition:

. . . God save the King! Will no one say Amen?
Am I both priest and clerk? Well then, Amen.

The actor takes centre stage for a dying soliloquy that to the onlookers seems endless. They can only stand helpless with embarrassment as Richard uncrowns himself. What does he gain from his theatrical antics? In the final analysis, he merely prolongs the agony for himself of handing over power to Bolingbroke.

In real life, the reign of Richard II was bedevilled by popular revolt and aristocratic punch-ups and he was thrown off the throne, not once, but twice. Four plays about the king, including Shakespeare's, appeared on the London stage during his lifetime, all dwelling on his incompetence, cronyism and the responsibility for the murder of his uncle, Thomas of Woodstock, the Duke of Gloucester.

But it was Shakespeare's play that got under the skin of Elizabeth I, for the parallels were plain for all to see. She, too, was accused of being misled by her favourites and flatterers, and Elizabeth immediately recognised the resemblance to herself. In her later years she faced both rebellion and dissent and is quoted as saying, 'I am Richard the Second, know ye not that?' and complained that 'a tragedy' of the king had been 'played forty times in open streets and houses'. The night before his attempted *putsch* in 1601, supporters of the Earl of Essex paid the Company of the Lord Chamberlain's Men to revive a play about 'the deposing and killing of Richard the Second' at The Globe Theatre. The performance took place as arranged, but Essex's attempted coup the following day was a cock-up and he was taken prisoner and beheaded. The parallels between Richard II and Elizabeth were so overt that the deposition scene was cut by the censors. For seven years performances of Richard II were given without its central and most riveting scene and it was only restored by James I and VI in 1608 after Elizabeth's death. It made for a strange play.

What do you call an uncrowned king? He is a king and not a king. 'God save King Henry? Unking'd Richard says'. And with the crown goes his very identity:

. . . I have no name, no title –
No, not that name was given me at the font –

> But 'tis usurped. Alack the heavy day,
> That I have worn so many winters out
> And know not now what name to call myself!
> (Act IV.1)

No name or not, you can't have an ex-king hanging around for too long. You never know who's going to suddenly get sentimental about the good old days. Enter Exton. Yet another fall guy to do the dirty work and keep the boss's hands clean.

Like a dog proudly bringing back a stick thrown by its master, Exton lays the body of Richard before Bolingbroke:

> EXTON: Great King, within this coffin I present
> Thy buried fear. Herein all breathless lies
> The mightiest of thy greatest enemies,
> Richard of Bordeaux, by me hither brought.

> KING HENRY: Exton, I thank thee not; for thou has wrought
> A deed of slander with thy fatal hand
> Upon my head and all this famous land.

> EXTON: From your own mouth, my lord, did I this deed.

> KING HENRY: They love not poison that do poison need;
> Nor do I thee. Though I did wish him dead,
> I hate the murderer, love him murderèd.
> The guilt of conscience take thou for thy labour,
> But neither my good word nor princely favour.
> With Cain go wander thorough shades of night,
> And never show thy head by day nor light.
> (Act V.6)

It's one thing to give the order, it's another to see the victim of that order gaping up at you. The king is appalled at being confronted with Richard's cadavre and launches immediately into a typical piece of Bolingbrokean back-sliding and evasion. It is significant that he changed his mind about imprisoning Richard in the Tower, diverting him to Pomfret when already on route to London. Better not to have him anywhere near the capital if an 'accident' happens, in case tongues wag. Better to be a long way away . . . We've seen it before: the indirect accusation of Richard over Thomas of Woodstock's death, which led to Bolingbroke challenging Mowbray to a duel, Later, in *Henry IV, Part 1*, we will see him avoid confrontation with Hotspur with an overt lie in order to bring him to heel. Now, we get another lie, a total denial of his involvement in the order to kill Richard. He looks Exton straight in the eye – 'They love not poison that do poison need.' If he were a rugby player, Bolingbroke would be continually penalised for coming in from the side. A vile politician indeed.

Thomas of Woodstock, is a valuable source of material for the characters of Bushy, Bagot and Green, notoriously under-written in *Richard II*, yet held by John of Gaunt, Bolingbroke and others to be the authors of Richard's being led astray, and his concomitant misuse of power. Bolingbroke has two of them executed. The problem is that these 'caterpillars of the Commonwealth' are so sketchily drawn that there is very little evidence of their crimes against the state on which to pin a convincing death penalty. Hence, there is a very peremptory trial with a number of accusations not borne out by the text, and off they are marched into history.

BOLINGBROKE: . . . You have misled a prince, a royal king,
A happy gentleman in blood and lineaments,
By you unhappied and disfigured clean.
You have in manner with your sinful hours
Made a divorce betwixt his Queen and him,
Broke the possession of a royal bed,
And stained the beauty of a fair queen's cheeks
With tears drawn from her eyes by your foul wrongs.
Myself – a prince by fortune of my birth,
Near to the King in blood, and near in love
Till you did make him misinterpret me –
Have stooped my neck under your injuries,
And sighed my English breath in foreign clouds,
Eating the bitter bread of banishment

> Whilst you have fed upon my signories,
> Disparked my parks, and felled my forest woods,
> From my own windows torn my household coat,
> Razed out my imprese, leaving me no sign
> Save men's opinions and my living blood
> To show the world I am a gentleman.
> This and much more, much more than twice all this,
> Condemns you to the death. See them delivered over
> To execution and the hand of death.
> (Act III.1)

Oh, dear! They've messed up his lawn, spoilt his hunting and kicked a ball through his favourite window. An ASBO, maybe, but beheading? Nor is the accusation that they've come between the queen and Richard borne out by the text. Quite the opposite. And as for giving Bolingbroke a bad name by loud-mouthing him to Richard with whom he professes to be bosom buddies, well . . . we have known such people who delude themselves as to the real nature of the truth; who believe something to be implicitly true at the moment that they say it simply *because* they say it. Falstaff springs to mind. When Bolingbroke wants something, any old excuse will do. It's a shame that we don't see more of Bushy, Bagot and Green. They disappear after Act II, Scene 2, paradoxically having aroused our sympathy. But if they are a problem so is Aumerle.

The scenes containing the Aumerle sub-plot., coming as they do right at the end of the play in Act V – between Richard on his way to the Tower and his murder – are palpably a dramatic device to hold the audience in suspense while waiting for the dénouement. The problem is asking us onlookers suddenly, at that stage in the play, to involve and interest ourselves in characters who only play supporting roles, merely to demonstrate a conspiracy against Bolingbroke. This is hardly balanced by having the chance to see the Duke of York willing to sacrifice his son Aumerle, as a traitor, thereby giving Bolingbroke the opportunity to demonstrate clemency. It's easy when the danger is so insignificant and the boy is so young. With the other conspirators, as with Bushey, Bagot and Green, Henry Bolingbroke is somewhat less than merciful. Dramatically, the incident is the calm before the storm, for immediately he orders the arrests of Aumerle's co-conspirators:

KING HENRY: But for our trusty brother-in-law and the Abbot,
With all the rest of that consorted crew,
Destruction straight shall dog them at the heels.
Good uncle, help to order several powers
To Oxford, or where'er these traitors are.
They shall not live within this world, I swear,
But I will have them if I once know where.
(Act V.3)

Then, in the next scene, he's killing Richard and banishing Exton. After all that, is it any wonder that he wants to go on a pilgrimage?

By the conclusion, Shakespeare has achieved something of a miracle in completely turning the tables on our feelings for Richard. He transforms him from a distasteful, selfish waster into someone for whom we have heartfelt sympathy. Or do we? Once a pig, always a pig. The trouble is, by the side of machiavellian Bolingbroke, Richard now looks positively angelic: the paradox of many of Shakespeare's falling tyrants is that they have a great deal more poetry in their souls than their conquerors: compare Macbeth and Malcolm. This aching gap between the pragmatism needed to rule and the power of the imagination to transcend earthly concerns is one which preoccupied Shakespeare, constantly baffling him. Man's inability to combine passion, poetry and humanity with the daily grind of taxation, unemployment, homelessness. Put like that, the difficulty seems obvious enough. 'If these things be necessities, let us treat them like necessities'. And so *real politik* rules and our hearts are left behind in the left luggage locker.

Towards the end of Richard's reign, it is impossible not to think of Richard's weaknesses somehow as strengths. In adversity, he cuts a much more humane figure than when he was king, his mind now unfettered and freed from those same problems of taxation and war. His downfall is orchestrated with impressive skill and, stripped of all office, he has time to confront his life and its shortcomings in some of the most intensely poetic passages of this most intensely lyrical play. In his final, long, last speech he muses on his misuse of his life. 'I did waste time, and now doth time waste me'.

. . . For now hath time made me his numbering clock.

My thoughts are minutes, and with sighs they jar
Their watches on unto mine eyes, the outward watch
Whereto my finger, like a dial's point,
Is pointing still in cleansing them from tears.
Now, sir, the sound that tells what hour it is
Are clamorous groans which strike upon my heart,
Which is the bell. So sighs, and tears, and groans
Show minutes, times, and hours. But my time
Runs posting on in Bolingbroke's proud joy,
While I stand fooling here, his jack of the clock.
(Act V.5)

He is now far from being 'glistering Phaeton', a sun King. He is not only down, he is out.

Down, down I come like glistering Phaeton,
Wanting the manage of unruly jades.
In the base court – base-court, where kings grow base
To come at traitors' calls, and do them grace.
In the base-court. Come down – down court, down King,
For night owls shriek where mounting larks should sing.
(Act III.3)

Richard's God has deserted him; all that is left behind is an impotent fool. Richard's dying words 'Exton, thy fierce hand/Hath with the king's blood stained the king's own land' are an ironic echo of the guilt with which Bolingbroke is left:

KING HENRY: . . . Lords, I protest, my soul is full of woe
That blood should sprinkle me to make me grow.
. . . I'll make a voyage to the Holy Land
To wash this blood off from my guilty hand.
(Act V.6)

Both Richard and King Henry, as he now is, are soaked in blood, blood which Henry will attempt to use to fertilise Gaunt's garden and make it grow again 'They love not poison that do poison need'.

Bolingbroke needed it all right, as he will need it again. It was the only route to becoming unequivocally king. But the guilt is now a monkey on his shoulder and the battle lines are drawn. For the next hundred years, far from healing England's wounds, Bolingbroke has set in motion a train of events that will lead to a surfeit of civil and internecine butchery as the ambition of two families turns Britain into the killing fields.

Notes

1.   Probably the same actor played Owen Glendower in *Henry IV, Part 1*. There is even a similarity of language.

The Henry IVs

Of a man who was mighty but wild as a boy,
O list to the ballad of Harry Le Roy

I don't buy Hal. He's a little shit. Sure, he makes some great war speeches but so did Churchill. When you're trying to persuade folks to get themselves killed to keep you in Mars Bars, it's amazing how the rhetoric flows. This 'star of England' embodies perfectly the dichotomy that Shakespeare finds in all rulers. The balancing act that they have to perform on the tight-rope of *real politik* and idealism; expediency wins out every time. Hal, unlike Macbeth, Richard III, Brutus, *et al*, doesn't let his imagination get a grip on him. He neatly sidesteps the pitfalls of ego and religion to emerge triumphantly at the end of *Henry V* with his reputation intact and France dangling at the end of his sword. How does he pull it all off without being rumbled?

There are two kinds of suspense drama. One where we are on the edge of our seats right until the last moment, waiting to find out whodunit. The other where we know the guilty party up front – either through a flash-back to the crime or through a self-confession. The *Henry IV*s fall into this latter category.

PRINCE HAL: I know you all, and will awhile uphold
The unyoked humour of your idleness.
Yet herein will I imitate the sun,
Who doth permit the base contagious clouds
To smother up his beauty from the world,
That when he please again to be himself,
Being wanted, he may be more wondered at
By breaking through the foul and ugly mists
Of vapours that did seem to strangle him.

> If all the year were playing holidays,
> To sport would be as tedious as to work;
> But when they seldom come, they wished-for come,
> And nothing pleaseth but rare accidents.
> So when this loose behaviour I throw off,
> And pay the debt I never promisèd,
> By how much better that my word I am,
> By so much shall I falsify men's hopes.
> And like bright metal on a sullen ground,
> My reformation, glittering o'er my fault,
> Shall show more goodly, and attract more eyes
> Than that which hath no foil to set it off.
> I'll so offend, to make offence a skill,
> Redeeming time when men think least I will.
> (Act I.2)

There it is, up front, a statement of intent. True or false? Is Hal the blagger of all time, wool-pulling over his and our eyes, a Mitty-esque figure fantasising about reforming his nature? There is no sense of irony in the speech, no petulant defiance, immaturity (though of course an actor could bring out all three of these characteristics). No – there is only the simple 'I know you all' – an objective appraisal of the intrinsic falsehood of the life he is leading and that at some point he will have to abandon. The gap year. Bumming it in Thailand. The losers will be his companions, those who are conned into believing that they have captured the ear of the future king and who will, at a Caligula-like stroke, fill positions in the law courts and treasury, instigate a Cade-like land where the pissing conduit will run with claret. Some hope.

Hal plays a long game. For close to eight hours we wait for the pay off. It comes at the conclusion of *Henry IV, Part 2* as the newly-crowned king, Henry V, chucks Falstaff out of his kingdom with the cursory couplet – 'I know thee not, old man. Fall to thy prayers.', Act V.5.

We search every moment of Hal's exploits with Falstaff, Poins, Pistol, Bardolph, and Peto for double meanings or a hidden agenda, forewarned with the knowledge that it's all a game; fascinated to see how he will pull it all off – will he/won't he? Is he just a loud-mouthed no-hoper? But because we know what's going on we look for the clues. At the climax at the Boar's

Head Tavern charade where Hal and Falstaff take turns to act out King and vassal (Act II.4), Falstaff says, 'Banish plump Jack, and banish all the world'. Hal replies 'I do, I will'. The signal for uncontrolled mirth and hilarity at the absurd proposition that when Hal is king he will get rid of his roistering companion in drink and sex? Or a chilly, prophetic indication of what *will* happen? No one in the bar knows. But we do.

Dodging, ducking, diving, weaving, Hal shimmies past desperate tackles, slips through outstretched arms to triumphantly touch down between the posts, leaving behind a trail of wrecked lives and the deaths of those with whom he purported to be friends; the rejection of a class of which he purported to be the champion, and whom he treats with contempt. Falstaff? Banish the fat slug. Bardolph? Hang him. 'We would have all such offenders so cut off'. Poins? Marry his sister? In yer dreams. 'Well, thus we play the fools with the time, and the spirits of the wise sit in the clouds and mock us.' Francis the drawer? Take the piss mercilessly, cruelly:

PRINCE HAL: . . . hark you, Francis, for the sugar thou gavest me, 'twas a pennyworth, was it not?

FRANCE: O Lord, I would it had been two!

PRINCE HAL: I will give thee for it a thousand pound – ask me when thou wilt, and thou shalt have it.

POINS: *(within)* **Francis!**

FRANCIS: Anon, anon.

PRINCE HAL: Anon, Francis? No, Francis, but tomorrow, France. Or Francis, a-Thursday. Or indeed Francis, when thou wilt. But Francis!

FRANCIS: My lord?

PRINCE HAL: Wilt thou rob this leathern-jerkin, crystal-button, not-pated, agate-ring, puke-stocking, caddis-garter,

> smooth-tongue Spanish pouch?
>
> FRANCIS: O Lord, sir, who do you mean?
>
> PRINCE HAL: Why then your brown bastard is your only drink. For look you, Francis, your white canvas doublet will sully. In Barbary, sir, it cannot come to so much.
>
> FRANCIS: What, sir?
>
> POINS: *(within)* Francis!
>
> PRINCE HAL: Away, you rogue, dost thou not hear them call? (Act II.4)

Ho, ho, a bundle of laughs. It's enough to make you ban hunting, not because of the fox but because of the hunter. A cruel exercise in class power. What on earth has the poor lad done to deserve such callous treatment? Quickly? Doll? Beat 'em up. Throw 'em in gaol. 'O God, that might should thus overcome right.' Williams? Humiliate him. Take no prisoners. In fact, if you do, kill 'em. Subjugate Kate. Crush France. No, I don't buy Hal.

Only Warwick (*Part 2*, Act IV.4) seems to have grasped Hal's tactics but his speech smacks as much of good hoodie psychoanalysis – the path of Marxist rebel to conservative billionaire – as of blinding insight into Hal's brat-pack behaviour. Maybe Bolingbroke/Henry IV was a bit too close to the wood:

> KING HENRY IV: Most subject is the fattest soil to weeds,
> And he, the noble image of my youth,
> Is overspread with them . . .
> The blood weeps from my heart when I do shape
> In forms imaginary th'unguided days
> And rotten times that you shall look upon
> When I am sleeping with my ancestors.
> For when this headstrong riot hath no curb,
> When rage and hot blood are his counsellors,

When means and lavish manners meet together,
O, with what wings shall his affections fly
Towards fronting peril and opposed decay!

WARWICK : My gracious lord, you look beyond him quite.
The Prince but studies his companions
Like a strange tongue, wherein, to gain the language,
'Tis needful that the most immodest word
Be looked upon and learnt, which, once attained,
Your highness knows, comes to no further use
But to be known and hated. So, like gross terms,
The Prince will, in the perfectness of time,
Cast off his followers, and their memory
Shall as a pattern or a measure live
By which his grace must mete the lives of other,
Turning past evils to advantages.
(*Part 2*, Act IV.4)

His speech repeats thought-for-thought Hal's opening soliloquy of almost two plays earlier, proof that when Will is up against it, a bit of recycling is in order.

Thus the path of Hal to the throne is a pre-meditated detour through the highways and by-ways of profligacy – one eye on the impression he makes on his yob companions, and the other a calculated assault on the rigid code of royal conduct that allows him to cock a snook at king and country while knowing that it will all end in conformity (now where have we seen all that before?)

'Let the end try the man'. 'Thus we play the fool with the time', Act IV.2. In *Henry IV, Part 2*, Act II.4, he is caught with his pants down. It costs nothing to play while the cat's away. But when the cat's at home . . .

PRINCE HENRY: Peto, how now, what news?

PETO: The King your father is at Westminster,
And there are twenty weak and wearied posts
Come from the north; and as I came along
I met and overtook a dozen captains,

> Bare-headed, sweating, knocking at the taverns,
> And asking every one for Sir John Falstaff.
>
> PRINCE HENRY: By heaven, Poins, I feel me much to blame,
> So idly to profane the precious time
> When tempest of commotion, like the south
> Borne with black vapour, doth begin to melt
> And drop upon our bare unarmèd heads.
> Give me my sword and cloak. Falstaff, good night.

And when the time is right he'll spring the surprise . . . obviously not after the Battle of Shrewsbury, where Falstaff claims to have killed Hotspur in Hal's place:

> PRINCE HAL: Why, Percy I killed myself, and saw thee dead.
>
> FALSTAFF: Didst thou? Lord, Lord, how this world is given to lying! I grant you I was down, and out of breath, and so was he, but we rose both at an instant, and fought a long hour by Shrewsbury clock. If I may be believed, so. If not, let them that should reward valour bear the sin upon their own heads. I'll take it upon my death, I gave him this wound in the thigh. If the man were alive, and would deny it, zounds, I would make him eat a piece of my sword.
>
> LANCASTER: This is the strangest tale that I ever heard.
>
> PRINCE HAL: This is the strangest fellow, brother John.
> (*Part 1*, Act V.4)

Brother John is sceptically standing by. Better to wait for a more opportune moment. Watch your back, Falstaff . . .

* * *

Who is Falstaff? What does he represent? Whether or not he is modelled on the real-life figure of Sir John Oldcastle, as the latter's family believed, thus occasioning a change of name for the character, Falstaff has come to embody all that is attractive in the Lord of Misrule. For a character who towers over the *Henry IV*s and who, even in death, casts a huge shadow over *Henry V*, he is a decidedly un-English character. His facility with language, colourful imagination and flights of wonderful fantasy, pissed or quasi-sober, are more reminiscent of Celts one has known. A Dylan Thomas or a Brendan Behan of an earlier Elizabethan era. But do you trust him? Charm and companionship ooze from him as he relieves you of your last fiver but you willingly stand him another pint merely to prise another story from his fertile imagination. How much of it was Shakespeare? Falstaff is akin to a stand-up routine, Burbage engaging, toying with, and confronting an audience with an improvised analysis of what motivates human behaviour. A one-on-one conversation that often rambles on beyond its time. Certainly, Shakespeare would not have written down everything that Falstaff says. There must have been an agreement between himself and Dick as to what the general gist of a soliloquy would be about and then Burbage would pick up the ball and run with it. A colloquy between a great writer and a great performer. But I bet Will had the last word.

Because underneath the lightness of the banter is a scurrilous villain whose behaviour is contemptible. It is no wonder that Hal, while ostensibly encouraging his antics, distances himself from the ultimate consequences while admitting to himself the attraction of such an opposite. There is no surprise in the demise of the fat fool, only the *frisson* of satisfaction in seeing the puffed-up, fantasising, self-aggrandising conman and coward get his comeuppance. Orson Welles captured perfectly the mean, sly, calculating quality of the character in *Chimes at Midnight*, the steel beyond the laughing eyes, the knife that wings its way towards your back, even as you share a glass. He robs and pillages and sends men to their graves without a second thought:

PRINCE HAL: . . . But tell me, Jack, whose fellows are these that come after?

FALSTAFF: Mine, Hal, mine.

PRINCE HAL: I did never see such pitiful rascals.

FALSTAFF: Tut, tut, good enough to toss, food for powder, food for powder, they'll fill a pit as well as better. Tush, man, mortal men, mortal men.
(*Part 1*, Act IV.2)

He recruits only the weak, the defenceless, the poor, the vulnerable, allowing the fit and strong to buy their way out of conscription.

SHALLOW: Come, Sir John, which four will you have?

FALSTAFF: Do you choose for me.

SHALLOW: Marry, then, Mouldy, Bullcalf, Feeble, and Shadow.

FALSTAFF: Mouldy and Bullcalf: for you, Mouldy, stay at home till you are past service; and for your part, Bullcalf, grow till you come unto it. I will none of you.

SHALLOW: Sir John, Sir John, do not yourself wrong; they are your likeliest men, and I would have you served with the best.

FALSTAFF: Will you tell me, Master Shallow, how to choose a man? Care I for the limb, the thews, the stature, bulk, and big assemblance of a man? Give me the spirit, Master Shallow. Here's Wart; you see what a ragged appearance it is. 'A shall charge you, and discharge you, with the motion of a pewterer's hammer, come off and on swifter than he that gibbets on the brewer's bucket. And this same half-faced fellow Shadow; give me this man; he presents no mark to the enemy – the foeman may with as great aim level at the edge of a penknife. And for a retreat, how swiftly will this Feeble the woman's tailor run off! O, give me the spare men, and spare me the great ones.
(*Part 2*, Act III.2)

Hospitality and friendship are mercilessly abused:

FALSTAFF: Master Shallow, I owe you a thousand pound.

SHALLOW: Yea marry, Sir John, which I beseech you to let me have home with me.

FALSTAFF: That can hardly be, Master Shallow. Do not you grieve at this.

And his credo is summed up in the great Honour speech:

FALSTAFF: . . . honour pricks me on. Yea, but how if honour prick me off when I come on, how then? Can honour set to a leg? No. Or an arm? No. Or take away the grief of a wound? No. Honour hath no skill in surgery then? No. What is honour? A word. What is in that word honour? What is that honour? Air. A trim reckoning! Who hath it? He that died a'Wednesday. Doth he feel it? No. Doth he hear it? No. 'Tis insensible, then? Yea, to the dead. But will it not live with the living? No. Why? Detraction will not suffer it. Therefore I'll none of it. Honour is a mere scutcheon – and so ends my catechism.
(*Part 1*, Act V.1)

The apparent truth of this pacifist statement marks the real truth behind its sentiment. That of the abject coward who achieves glory by slashing a wound in a dead man's thigh and claims the victory as his.

The better part of valour is discretion, in the which better part I have saved my life. Zounds, I am afraid of this gunpowder Percy, though he be dead. How if he should counterfeit too and rise? By my faith, I am afraid he would prove the better counterfeit. Therefore I'll make him sure, yea, and I'll swear I killed him. Why may not he rise as well as I? Nothing confutes me but eyes, and nobody sees me. Therefore, sirrah (*stabbing him*), with a new wound in your

thigh, come you along with me.
(Act V.4)

No. No matter which way you turn him, Falstaff is, despite his snake-like fascination, a deeply unattractive character.

* * *

Henry IV, Parts 1 and *2* follow a similar structural pattern in alternating court and low-life scenes, and together they form the most complete State of the British Nation picture in dramatic history, capable as they are of a myriad of mirror images of UK life at any point in the last six hundred years. Understandably, *Henry IV, Part 1* is more performed, studied and popular than *Henry IV, Part 2*. Logical, really – nobody goes to just see Part Two of anything, but with Part One you are in at the beginning of the story. I studied Part One for 'O' Level, and played Poins in a school production. We went to see a rival version performed by Alleyn's School and were shocked at the sight of boys in dresses humping on a table in the Boar's Head Tavern. The fifties were a time of Hank Jansen under the bedclothes, measuring each other behind the bicycle sheds, Health and Efficiency in a brown wrapper. Overt sexuality was embarrassing. Yet the *Henrys* are riddled with raunch and can be studied today in a way that was closed to us then, callow, smutty schoolboys that we were. Similarly, we are no longer impaled on a gung ho imperial spike that refuses to countenance anything other than royalty as deity. My Country Right or Wrong. Do or Die. The immediate post-war period was a monarchist's heaven.

How wild exactly was Henry? The problem is that despite numerous reports about his behaviour, we do not actually see him do anything. No binge drinking, mugging, joy-riding. Not all hoodies are criminals, it's just being one of the boys. His misdemeanours – apart from the 'vile company' he keeps – rest on one incident only. In the anonymous *The Famous Victories of Henry V*, written in about 1580, he has a punch-up with the Lord Chief Justice.

The action covers both Henry's wild youth, in which he is a very boisterous madcap prince indeed, and the famous victories of the title, culminating in the wooing of Princess Katherine of France.

Shakespeare chose not to show the scene from the *Famous Victories* when, in defence of a palpably guilty thief, Thomas Cutter, one of his servants, Hal fetches the Lord Chief Justice one about the ear in court, for refusing to release Cutter. For this, Hal is sent to prison and from such stuff legends grow. In *Henry IV, Part 2*, we get a reference only to this when the page announces the Lord Chief Justice's arrival with 'Here comes the nobleman that committed the Prince for striking him about Bardolph.', Act I.2. Thus, Cutter mutates into Bardolph, seen throughout *Henry IV, Part 1* and at the beginning of *Henry IV, Part 2*, as something of Hal's servant. This prepares the way for Hal's brutal treatment of Bardolph in *Henry V*, where, in France, he has him hanged for stealing 'a pax of little price' from a church.

The Lord Chief Justice affair acts as a useful springboard for others to lament Hal's profligacy and add flesh to the wild legend. Twice, Bolingbroke/Henry IV lets off a diatribe against his son, comparing him unfavourably with the Earl of Northumberlan'd son, Hotspur, and on his deathbed he raises an apocalyptic vision of a Britain cursed with Hal's behaviour.

> **KING HENRY IV: . . . What, canst thou not forbear me half**
> **an hour?**
> Then get thee gone, and dig my grave thyself,
> And bid the merry bells ring to thine ear
> That thou art crownèd, not that I am dead.
> Let all the tears that should bedew my hearse
> Be drops of balm to sanctify they head;
> Only compound me with forgotten dust.
> Give that which gave thee life unto the worms.
> Pluck down my officers, break my decrees;
> For now a time is come to mock at form –
> Harry the Fifth is crowned! Up, vanity!
> Down, royal state! All you sage counsellors, hence!
> And to the English court assemble now,
> From every region, apes of idleness!
> Now, neighbour confines, purge you of your scum!
> Have you a ruffian that will swear, drink, dance,
> Revel the night, rob, murder, and commit

> The oldest sins the newest kind of ways?
> Be happy, he will trouble you no more.
> England shall double gild his treble guilt;
> England shall give him office, honour, might;
> For the fifth Harry from curbed licence plucks
> The muzzle of restraint, and the wild dog
> Shall flesh his tooth on every innocent.
> O my poor kingdom, sick with civil blows!
> When that my care could not withhold thy riots,
> What wilt thou do when riot is thy care?
> O, thou wilt be a wilderness again,
> Peopled with wolves, thy old inhabitants!
> (*Part 2*, Act IV.5)

But to what does Hal's behaviour in the plays *actually* amount? He refuses to take part in the Gad's Hill robbery, instead robbing Falstaff and the boys of their ill-gotten gains and returning the booty to the unfortunate pilgrims with a little bit of extra for their trouble ('The money shall be paid back again with advantage', Act II.4). We see him defy the Lord's Chief Justice when it costs him nothing (Act II.4). We see him enjoying common company but we never see him drunk. There is no sense that he joins in the whoring and indeed, until Katherine at the end of *Henry V*, he doesn't go anywhere near a woman. I am still waiting for the first English gay Hal, as in the Dutch director Luc Percival's psychodrama productions, *Schlachten* at the Deutscheschauspielhaus, Hamburg, in 2000. The timid, gentle, homosexual Hal is forced by his father through disparaging comparisons with the hot-headed, war-mongering butchness of Hotspur into a demonstration of hyper-masculinity. Roland Renner, a member of my Schauspielhaus company when I was Intendant (Chief Executive) for four years, played Falstaff as an ageing queen – more Danny La Rue than Orson Welles. The relationship of an old man in love with a young boy was always going to end in tears. Cross-dressing and the sexual ambiguity contained therein have led us in the 21st century to mine the plays more openly for their homosexual content in ways that would have been taboo in past centuries. Jonathan Goldberg, in 'Hal's Desire, Shakespeare's Idaho'[1] is another to advance the theory of the 'bed-presser' Falstaff and Hal as lovers. It's a theory. But try as one will to inject fucking and fighting into the story a pure reading of the text comes up with Hal merely the observer of others' behaviour, summed up in *Henry IV, Part 2*, Act II.4, where Hal and Poins dress up as tapsters in the Boars Head Tavern to overhear what Falstaff is saying about them (shades of Diana and Fergy in police outfits, blagging their way undetected into a night club). This is the perfect image of Hal's projection of himself as a member of the lower orders. His mind can never get beyond the sense of himself playing a part, standing outside the class to which he has loaned his body if not his mind. Every act, every statement, must be disguised. He can never be himself. The true Hal is only revealed in instinctive flashes, where his guard drops and the ruthless cynic is revealed. A pragmatic chip off the old Bolingbroke block. 'If these things be necessities, then let us treat them like necessities'. For Hal, the necessity is to pretend to be wild until the black crow turns into an exotic bird of paradise.

I also don't buy into the idea that Hal's behaviour is the typical adolescent phase of a teenager rebelling against his father whilst serving an apprenticeship for the crown. This is a Tillyard inherited view[2], still peddled by those who studied under or are influenced by his disciples. Hence Michael Billington in *The Guardian* reviewing Nick Hytner's productions of *Henry IV, Parts 1* and *2* at The Royal National Theatre:

> . . . a story of the education of a prince . . . in Hynter's hands
> . . . a study of a son, desperate to engage his father's love.

It would be, if we didn't have that calculated speech up front to tell us otherwise. Take Claudius' confession speech out of *Hamlet*, 'O my offence is rank', and you would never know whether he had committed the murder or not. Interesting. Nevertheless, the situation is complicated by Hal's relationship with his father – Henry Bolingbroke, Henry IV – which is founded on the quintessential parental disappointment in what appears to be an under-achieving elder son. Hal didn't make the First IX, not like Hotspur.

KING HENRY: . . . there thou makest me sad, and makest me sin

In envy that my Lord Northumberland
Should be the father to so blest a son:
A son who is the theme of honour's tongue,
Amongst a grove the very straightest plant,
Who is sweet Fortune's minion and her pride –
Whilst I by looking on the praise of him
See riot and dishonour stain the brow
Of my young Harry. O that it could be proved
That some night-tripping fairy had exchanged
In cradle-clothes our children where they lay,
And called mine Percy, his Plantagenet!
Then would I have his Harry, and he mine.
(Act I.1)

And then later:

Why, Harry, do I tell thee of my foes,
Which art my nearest and dearest enemy?
Thou art like enough, thorough vassal fear,
Base inclination, and the start of spleen,
To fight against me under Percy's pay,
To dog his heels, and curtsy at his frowns,
To show how much thou art degenerate.
(Act III.2)

Push a boy too hard in one direction and the chances are he'll
charge off in the other. Chess, cricket and philosophy? Nah – sex,
drugs and rock 'n' roll. But I'll surprise you, says Hal in an echo of his
first soliloquy, when you least expect it. I'll sort it out:

Do not think it so, you shall not find it so;
And God forgive them that so much have swayed
Your majesty's good thoughts away from me!
I will redeem all this on Percy's head,
And in the closing of some glorious day
Be bold to tell you that I am your son . . .
If not, the end of life cancels all bonds,

And I will die a hundred thousand deaths
Ere break the smallest parcel of this vow.
(Act III.2)

If there is a trace of historical fact left in the plays of the legend of the wild prince, it may be in the relationship with his father. In reality, Hal was much closer to the decision-making process of the court than the plays depict. The impression that he spent all his days whooping it up are a false one and as King Henry became increasingly ill Hal – Prince Henry – took more and more control of the council, packing it with associates and chums of his own – a situation that mirrored Richard II, and one of the very reasons why Bolingbroke usurped the crown in the first place. Prince Henry became so powerful that it was even mooted that the king abdicate in favour of his son. Henry's reaction to this suggestion was characteristically swift and decisive, when without warning he peremptorily dismissed Hal and his pals from the council. Hal's brother, Thomas of Clarence, was installed in his place and there remains a reference to this incident in *Henry IV, Part I*, Act III.2, when in the midst of giving Hal a bollocking for his behaviour the king says, 'Thy place in Council thou has rudely lost,/Which by thy younger brother is supplied'. Shakespeare's change in emphasis from the historical is that the dismissal is attributed to Hal's wildness rather than his political ambition, the sense of which is non-existent outside his opening soliloquy.

Historically, Hal was only sixteen at the time of the Battle of Tewkesbury, and, needing no ID card to prove his age, was already into a binge-drinking culture in a way that today's youth would have envied. Such a charismatic young heir apparent to the throne with a penchant for painting the town red naturally would have attracted much attention and a group of companions would have grown up around him. Whether these would have included a surrogate father-figure in a Falstaff is another matter, but certainly a bunch of hangers-on who were the antithesis of the sober king and his courtiers. Holinshed, the source of the father/son relationship has two stories concerning the estrangement of Hal and Henry and their ultimate reconciliation. The first is the story where Hal, mistakenly thinking his father dead, takes the crown from his pillow and tries it on for size:

. . . My gracious lord! My father!
This sleep is sound indeed; this is a sleep
That from this golden rigol hath divorced
So many English kings. Thy due from me
Is tears and heavy sorrows of the blood,
Which nature, love, and filial tenderness
Shall, O dear father, pay thee plenteously.
My due from thee is this imperial crown,
Which, as immediate from thy place and blood,
Deserves itself to me.

He puts the crown on his head.

Lo, where it sits,
Which God shall guard, and put the world's whole strength
Into one giant arm, it shall not force
This lineal honour from me. This from thee
Will I to mine leave, as 'tis left to me.
(*Part 2*, Act IV.5)

The second story which appears in *The Famous Victories* and which surprisingly Shakespeare did not use is one of Hal's appearance before his father in the midst of Council with a group of followers, all dressed in 'strange apparell'. Drawing a knife and proffering it to Bolingbroke à la Richard III and Anne, he asks the king to kill him if he suspects him of being disloyal: 'The king moved herewith, cast from him the dagger, and embracing the prince kissed him, and with shedding tears confessed, that in deed he had him partlie in suspicion, though now (as he perceived) not with just cause, and therefore from thencefoorth no misreport should cause him to have him in mistrust'[3]. We get a suggestion of this when, at Henry's accusation that Hal is intending to join with the rebels and fight on Harry Percy's side, Hal throws up his hands in horror and says, 'Do not think it so, you shall not find it so; And God forgive them that so much have swayed/Your majesty's good thoughts away from me!', Act III.2. He calls these gossips 'smiling pickthanks and base newsmongers'. The fact remains, though, that to Henry it looks as if Hal has been caught with his pants down, red-handedly appropriating the crown. Hal must convince his father of the genuineness of his tears. He gives the crown back:

> **. . . There is your crown,**
> **And He that wears the crown immortally**
> **Long guard it yours! If I affect it more**
> **Than as your honour and as your renown,**
> **Let me no more from this obedience rise . . .**
> **(Act IV.5)**

Thus king and son are reconciled for a second time – the first a temporary moment when he saves the king's life at the hands of the Douglas at the Battle of Shrewsbury, a moment undermined by Falstaff claiming victory over Hotspur, thus leaving the way open for the estrangement in Part Two. The fact that as long ago as *Richard II*, we have learnt that Bolingbroke hasn't seen his son for some time – 'Can no man tell me of my unthrifty son? 'Tis full some time since I did see him last' – only serves to underline the gulf that has grown between them and the theatrical neglect of Hal's courtly duties that Shakespeare has inserted into the story.

What father would not want a son like Hotspur? Brave, blunt, forthright, honest. But could he lead a country? It's the old Shakespeare dichotomy. You may want the Harry Percys to be in charge but the place would soon be in chaos. Too many risks taken, the heart ruling the head; too much nose off-cutting for face-spiting. No, you need a cool pragmatist weighing up the options. A 'vile politician'. A Bolingbroke. A Hal . . . It's superficially attractive to have a valiant warrior who fights fair, believes in a chivalric code, particularly when your back is to the wall. But fairness never won wars. A Macbeth to save a Duncan. A Macduff to do the dirty work. And in times of peace? No. Hotspur is a rebel, sometimes with, sometimes without, a cause and there is an argument for believing that Hal is able to defeat him because where, for Hotspur, the duel is a trial of fighting skill, for Hal to win is a psychological imperative. His determination is stronger, his need is greater:

> **And God forgive them that so much have swayed**
> **Your majesty's good thoughts away from me!**

I will redeem all this on Percy's head,
And in the closing of some glorious day
Be bold to tell you that I am your son,
When I will wear a garment all of blood,
And stain my favours in a bloody mask,
Which, washed away, shall scour my shame with it.
And that shall be the day, whene'er it lights,
That this same child of honour and renown,
This gallant Hotspur, this all-praisèd knight,
And your unthought-of Harry chance to meet.
For every honour sitting on his helm,
Would they were multitudes, and on my head
My shames redoubled. For the time will come
That I shall make this northern youth exchange
His glorious deeds for my indignities.
Percy is but my factor, good my lord,
To engross up glorious deeds on my behalf,
And I will call him to so strict account
That he shall render every glory up,
Yea, even the slightest worship of his time,
Or I will tear the reckoning from his heart.
This in the name of God I promise here,
The which if He be pleased I shall perform,
I do beseech your majesty may salve
The long-grown wounds of my intemperance.
If not, the end of life cancels all bonds,
And I will die a hundred thousand deaths
Ere break the smallest parcel of this vow.
(Act III. 2)

And he does exactly that.

* * *

Three male characters dominate the eight-play cycle. Bolingbroke/
Henry IV, whose spurt for the tape begins the whole cycle in *Richard II*,
before dying at the end of *Henry IV, Part 2*, passing the baton onto his

son: Hal/Henry V, who runs through three plays and is heard about in the fourth (*Richard II*) and Richard of Gloucester; Richard III, who starts his ascent in *Henry VI, Part 2*. We may add to this trio a female fourth – Queen Margaret, Margaret of Anjou, whose formidable march through the plays parallels Richard's, interlocking and interweaving her fate with his, a Nemesis figure, a fury, whose Chorus-like prophesies are fulfilled in a way reminiscent of the witches in *Macbeth*.

Bolingbroke is the cautious counterpart to Richard III, marking out his territory, sweeping the ground for mines and only advancing when he is sure of his position. But the burden of guilt that he feels is one that he carries with him throughout his reign, even as he commits more crimes to keep him on the throne.

> **. . . God knows, my son,**
> **By what by-paths and indirect crooked ways**
> **I met this crown . . .**
> (***Part 2**, Act IV.5*)

Acquiring the crown illegitimately and then getting rid of Richard II has given him such a deep-rooted complex that he feels that the only way he can atone is to go on a crusade to fight the infidel. As if that will make it all right. The lasting legacy of the crusades is the schism today that exists between Christianity and Islam – the seemingly irreconcilable differences stemming from this abject period of our colonial history. *Henry IV, Part 1* begins immediately with Bolingbroke's stated intention:

> **. . . Therefore friends,**
> **As far as to the sepulchre of Christ –**
> **Whose soldier now, under whose blessed cross**
> **We are impressèd and engaged to fight –**
> **Forthwith a power of English shall we levy,**
> **Whose arms were moulded in their mother's womb**
> **To chase these pagans in those holy fields**
> **Over whose acres walked those blessed feet,**
> **Which fourteen hundred years ago were nailed**
> **For our advantage on the bitter cross.**
> (*Act I.1*)

Two plays later, on his deathbed, he is still trying to get there. But his purpose is clear. It was all a ruse to divert attention from problems at home. A trip to the Holy Land is just an excuse to mask his insecurity and keep his critics and opponents quiet. So watch yourself, he says to Hal, and take a leaf out of my book. His dying advice to Hal sums up as succinctly as anything he says the way his mind never ceases to operate on the political level.

> Yet thou standest more sure than I could do,
> Thou art not firm enough, since griefs are green;
> And all my friends, which thou must make thy friends,
> Have but their stings and teeth newly ta'en out,
> By whose fell working I was first advanced,
> And by whose power I well might lodge a fear
> To be again displaced; which to avoid,
> I cut them off, and had a purpose now
> To lead out many to the Holy Land,
> Lest rest and lying still might make them look
> Too near unto my state. Therefore, my Harry,
> Be it thy course to busy giddy minds
> With foreign quarrels, that action hence borne out . . .
> (Act IV.5)

Divert your enemies away from the problems at home with a trumped-up war of expediency. And Hal does just that. His old dad's advice holds good.

Rally the country round the flag – it's amazing what it will do for your popularity. It seems that this bellicose jingoistic streak runs deep in the British psyche, for 600 years later Thatcher triumphed in exactly the same way. Heading for disaster in the polls, she headed for The Falklands and returned to win a resounding victory in the following election. Blair tried the same trick and despite ferocious opposition stirred up by the illegitimacy of the war in Iraq, some 75% of the population were nevertheless in favour of aggressively toppling Sadaam Hussein. Despite being severely economical with the truth, Blair still managed to win an unprecedented third term of government for the Labour party. What is it about war that brings out the worst? Sanguine, rational people succumb to the rush of adrenalin that the sound of drum and shell stir in the blood, losing all sense of proportion. And they kid themselves that a particular cause is just, flying in the teeth of incontrovertible evidence. 'Busy giddy minds with foreign quarrels'. Bolingbroke was there 600 years ago. But he never did get to the Holy Land. He was conned by some tea leaf reader into thinking that was where he'd meet his maker, but like Birnham Wood, it was a trick. He died in the Jerusalem Room of the Palace.

* * *

There was at least one Welshman in Shakespeare's company of actors – on occasions, two, and a father and son who were Welsh-speaking. It is possible to trace the paths of these players through the thirty seven plays – from *Henry IV, Part 1* right through to *Cymbeline*, one of his last plays, and examine both the stereotypes and the prejudices. Voluble, emotional and given to saying 'Look you', nevertheless there is an appreciation of the Welsh and Welsh culture that belies the reputation of later centuries. It is clear that in the Tudor court the Welsh had great standing and with such a champion as Shakespeare to defend them it is a mystery as to why the people of this small country have, until very recently, endured racial ridicule and suffered the suppression of their language, one of the oldest in Europe.

In the midst of the Machiavellian mayhem of the rebels Northumberland and Glendower dividing England into three parts comes one of the most heart-rending and beautiful scenes in the whole of the canon. Edmund Mortimer, an heir to the throne, whose persona Shakespeare condenses from two characters of the same name, has been taken prisoner by Owen Glendower. There he falls in love with Glendower's daughter and marries her. Only one problem – she can speak no English, he no Welsh:

MORTIMER: This is the deadly spite that angers me,
My wife can speak no English, I no Welsh.

And then Glendower translates what Lady Mortimer says:

GLENDOWER: My daughter weeps, she will not part with you,

She'll be a soldier too, she'll to the wars.

MORTIMER: Good father, tell her that she and my aunt Percy
Shall follow in your conduct speedily.

Glendower speaks to her in Welsh, and she answers him in the same.

GLENDOWER: She is desperate here, a peevish self-willed
harlotry, one that no persuasion can do good upon.

The lady speaks in Welsh.
(Act III.1)

It is noticeable that the Welsh has not survived the transposition
into the quarto or the folio editions – a non Welsh-speaking stage
manager. Not uncommon outside of Wales. All we have is a series of
stage directions: *'The lady speaks in Welsh'. 'The lady speaks again in
Welsh'. 'Here, the lady sings a Welsh song'.* Obviously, there was a
whole scene in which both she and her father, Glendower, speak in
Welsh with each other, which has been lost to us but which probably
the actor playing Glendower composed. Any production worth its salt
has to invent such a scene.[4] Mortimer can only look on impotently:

MORTIMER: I understand thy looks, that pretty Welsh
Which thou pourest down from these swelling heavens
I am too perfect in and, but for shame
In such a parley I should answer thee.

The lady speaks again in Welsh.

I understand thy kisses, and thou mine,
And that's a feeling disputation,
But I will never be a truant, love,
Till I have learnt thy language, for thy tongue
Makes Welsh as sweet as ditties highly penned,
Sung by a fair queen in a summer's bower
With ravishing division to her lute.

GLENDOWER: Nay, if you melt, then will she run mad.
The lady speaks again in Welsh.

MORTIMER: O, I am ignorance itself in this!
(Act III.1)

Here, in one short scene, is the proof of Shakespeare's extraordinary all-embracing humanity and tolerance. The language is beautiful, Mortimer will learn it. No matter that English is the language spoken by the majority. The young Welsh-speaking boy who played the role of Glendower's daughter found himself in one of the theatre's earliest and most quintessential pleas for racial, linguistic and cultural tolerance. A man who could write such a scene and with such an understanding of cultural difference can never be accused of anti-semitism in the writing of *The Merchant of Venice*, or chauvinistic misogyny in *The Taming of the Shrew*. Once a humanist, always a humanist. Four centuries later, Brian Friel repeated the situation in *Translations*, a play about the love of a British soldier and a young Irish-speaking peasant girl.

The bardic figure of Owen Glendower, his language fired with myth and poetic imagination, has traditionally been the butt of much ridicule, mocked and jeered at for his bombast and portentousness, an early Welsh windbag. But Shakespeare is not dealing here in stereotypes. We only have to look at his treatment of the English in the same scene. Glendower is confronted by the more prosaic and down-to-earth scepticism of the Geordie Hotspur. The cultural eloquence of the Welsh versus the linguistic philistinism of the English – a polarisation of the two cultures that exists to this day. Was Shakespeare's tongue planted firmly in his cheek?

MORTIMER: Fie, cousin Percy, how you cross my father!

HOTSPUR: I cannot choose. Sometime he angers me
With telling me of the moldwarp and the ant,
Or the dreamer Merlin and his prophecies,
And of a dragon and a finless fish,
A clip-winged griffin and a moulten raven,
A couching lion and a ramping cat,

And such a deal of skimble-skamble stuff
As puts me from my faith. I tell you what –
He held me last night at least nine hours
In reckoning up the several devils' names
That were his lackeys. I cried 'Hum', and 'Well, go to!'
But marked him not a word. O, he is as tedious
As a tired horse, a railing wife,
Worse than a smoky house. I had rather live
With cheese and garlic in a windmill, far,
Than feed on cates and have him talk to me
In any summer house in Christendom.
(Act III.1)

A direct clash – Anglo-Saxon versus Celt. Lady Mortimer sings a song in Welsh (see Appendix II):

GLENDOWER: She bids you on the wanton rushes lay you down,
And rest your gentle head upon her lap,
And she will sing the song that pleaseth you,
And on your eyelids crown the god of sleep . . .

Hotspur, immediately jealous of Lady Mortimer's talent, makes a series of crude sexual jokes full of double meaning, using his wife as a butt:

HOTSPUR: Come, Kate, thou art perfect in lying down.
Come, quick, quick, that I may lay my head in thy lap.

LADY PERCY: Go, ye giddy goose.

And it gets worse:

LADY PERCY: Lie still, ye thief, and hear the lady sing in Welsh.

HOTSPUR: I had rather hear Lady my brach howl in Irish.

LADY PERCY: Wouldst thou have thy head broken?

HOTSPUR: No.

LADY PERCY: Then be still.

HOTSPUR: Neither, 'tis a woman's fault.

LADY PERCY: Now, God help thee!

HOTSPUR: To the Welsh lady's bed.

LADY PERCY: What's that?

HOTSPUR: Peace, she sings.

Here the lady sings a Welsh song.

What is he doing? Why won't he keep still? Is he trying to burrow under Lady Percy's skirt? Hotspur immediately wishes to offer up his wife in competition. He's had enough of this Celtic mysticism and what he sees as effete cultural affectation. And as his resentment grows so the positions become even more polarised. The Hotspur that defied Bolingbroke because he took a dislike to his effete envoy because he was:

> **. . . perfumèd like a milliner,**
> **And 'twixt his finger and his thumb he held**
> **A pouncet-box, which ever and anon**
> **He gave his nose, and took it away again . . .**
> **(Act I.3)**

now turns his Philistine guns on the Glendower household:

HOTSPUR: . . . Come, Kate, I'll have your song too.

LADY PERCY: Not mine, in good sooth.

HOTSPUR: Not yours, in good sooth! Heart, you swear like a comfit-maker's wife – 'Not you, in good sooth!', and 'As true

as I live!', and 'As God shall mend me!', and 'As sure as day!' –
And givest such sarcenet surety for thy oaths
As if thou never walkest further than Finsbury.
Swear me, Kate, like a lady as thou art,
A good mouth-filling oath, and leave 'In sooth',
And such protest of pepper-gingerbread,
To velvet-guards, and Sunday citizens.
Come, sing.

LADY PERCY: I will not sing.
(Act III.1)

Language should be short, blunt and not more than two syllables and preferably contain an oath every other word. Hotspur would have been at home in today's dumbed-down yob culture, where 'fuck' has become a *de rigeur* appendage to every descriptive epithet. He digs a linguistic hole for himself, out of which he is unable to climb with dignity. All this amidst the medieval equivalent of Potsdam.

Geoffrey of Monmouth, in his *Histories of the Kings of Britain*, recounts the story of the division of Britain into three parts during the reign of *Lir*. This becomes the springboard both for Shakespeare's play *King Lear* and for the defeat of the rebels in *Henry IV, Part 1*.

GLENDOWER: Come, here is the map, shall we divide our right
According to our threefold order taken?

MORTIMER: The archdeacon hath divided it
Into three limits very equally.
England, from Trent and Severn hitherto,
By south and east is to my part assigned.
All westward, Wales beyond the Severn shore,
And all the fertile land within that bound,
To Owen Glendower. And, dear coz, to you
The remnant northward, lying off from Trent . . .

HOTSPUR: Methinks my moiety, north from Burton here,

In quantity equals not one of yours.
See how this river comes me cranking in,
And cuts me from the best of all my land
A huge half-moon, a monstrous cantle out.
I'll have the current in this place damm'd up,
And here the smug and silver Trent shall run
In a new channel, fair and evenly.
It shall not wind with such a deep indent,
To rob me of so rich a bottom here.

GLENDOWER: Not wind? It shall, it must – you see it doth.
. . .

HOTSPUR: I'll have it so, a little charge will do it.

GLENDOWER: I'll not have it altered.

HOTSPUR: Will not you?

GLENDOWER: No, nor you shall not.

HOTSPUR: Who shall say me nay?

GLENDOWER: Why, that will I.

HOTSPUR: Let me not understand you, then, speak it in Welsh.

GLENDOWER: I can speak English, lord, as well as you,
For I was trained up in the English court,
Where, being but young, I framèd to the harp
Many an English ditty lovely well,
And gave the tongue a helpful ornament –
A virtue that was never seen in you.

HOTSPUR: . . . I had rather hear a brazen candle-stick turned,
Or a dry wheel grate on the axle-tree,
And that would set my teeth nothing on edge,

Nothing so much as mincing poetry.
'Tis like the forced gait of a shuffling nag.

GLENDOWER: Come, you shall have Trent turned.
(Act III.1)

The attempt founders on that old rock of dispute, national boundaries. West Bank, Alsace-Lorraine, Poland partition, Cyprus, Uganda, Rwanda, the Congo, Somalia – in fact, anywhere in Africa – the farmer's fence encroaching one metre into the neighbour's meadow, the overhanging tree . . . history is littered with the corpses of shattered agreements, victims of greed and avarice, the territorial imperative. Have Trent turned? Patently ridiculous. But the failure of Percy, Glendower and Mortimer to amicably resolve the frightening division of the land into three parts leads irrevocably to disarray and defeat as first Northumberland and then Glendower fail to turn up for the match. Wisely, it would appear, for where in *Henry IV, Part 1* civil dispute at Shrewsbury is resolved in the traditional battle of armies in a one-to-one combat culminating in the ultimate contest of leader against leader for the glory of the crown, here in *Henry IV, Part 2* the Battle of Tewkesbury is won without a single shot being fired. Prince John, a true younger chip off the old Bolingbroke block, outwits the rebels with a false promise of peace, arrests them when their armies disperse and then has them beheaded. A masterly piece of *real politik* heralding the onset of pragmatic rule and the death of the chivalric code embodied in the heroics of Hotspur:

ARCHBISHOP: Will you thus break your faith?

PRINCE JOHN: I pawned thee none.
I promised you redress of these same grievances
Whereof you did complain, which, by mine honour,
I will perform with a most Christian care.
But, for you rebels, look to taste the due
Meet for rebellion and such acts as yours.
Most shallowly did you these arms commence,
Fondly brought here, and foolishly sent hence.

Strike up our drums, pursue the scattered stray;
God, and not we, hath safely fought today.
Some guard these traitors to the block of death,
Treason's true bed and yielder-up of breath.
(*Part 2*, Act IV.2)

However much Bolingbroke may have longed for a *soupçon* of Percy in Hal, it is surely John's tactics that he admired most. We catch a glimpse of this family trait, which Hal is to exploit so ruthlessly when he comes to the throne, in Bolingbroke's first encounter with Hotspur, where he outrageously and perfidiously denies Hotspur's claims to keep his prisoners.

HOTSPUR: Revolted Mortimer!
He never did fall off, my sovereign liege,
But by the chance of war. To prove that true
Needs no more but one tongue for all those wounds,
Those mouthèd wounds, which valiantly he took,
When on the gentle Severn's sedgy bank,
In single opposition hand to hand,
He did confound the best part of an hour
In changing hardiment with great Glendower.
Three times they breathed, and three times did they drink
Upon agreement of swift Severn's flood,
Who then affrighted with their bloody looks
Ran fearfully among the trembling reeds,
And hid his crisp head in the hollow bank,
Bloodstainèd with these valiant combatants.
Never did bare and rotten policy
Colour her working with such deadly wounds,
Nor never could the noble Mortimer
Receive so many, and all willingly.
Then let him not him be slandered with revolt.

KING HENRY: Thou dost belie him, Percy, thou dost belie him,
He never did encounter with Glendower.
I tell thee, he durst as well have met the devil alone

> **As Owen Glendower for an enemy.**
> **Art thou not ashamed? But sirrah, henceforth**
> **Let me not hear you speak of Mortimer.**
> **(*Part 1*, Act 1.3)**

With so admired a son, a role model for the English youth, why does Northumberland betray Harry Percy, refusing to turn up for the match at Shrewsbury, leaving the team a key striker short? He must know that he is condemning him to probable death.

> **Fain would I go to meet the Archbishop,**
> **But many thousand reasons hold me back.**
> **(*Part 2*, Act II.3)**

Maybe as Hal's behaviour is a reaction against his father's parenting methods, so Hotspur's bravery is an instinctive reaction against his father's cowardice. Both sons defy their fathers and represent as they do the two faces of the same coin.

What sort of land would it have been if the rebels had succeeded? Probably a land that would pretty soon have descended into chaos as rival factions fought with each other over possession and splinter groups formed radical movements to out-manoeuvre each other. An Anglo-Saxon equivalent of a medieval Italy – fiefdoms everywhere, back to the feuding era of the Celtic tribes. It's a good job that the rebels behaved like squabbling war lords, Britain would have been changed irrevocably. (Wales might have thrived though). Britain today is *en route* to federalism, devolution achieving peacefully what 600 years ago was attempted by force. Even so, it is amazing how many of the old grievances and attitudes are still prevalent. The Scots, the Welsh and the Northern Irish find it hard to erase the memory of 600 years of English oppression., their countries still, when the chips are down, under Westminster rule.

Notes

1. *Theory and Practice*, Ed Nigel Wood.
2. *The Elizabethan World Picture*, EMW Tillyard, 1943.
3. Bullough, IV.
4. I offer up a possible example in Appendix I.

Henry V

This star of England

Henry V, a charismatic chameleon. Charming but ruthless. Coldness behind the eyes, one aspect that Olivier got right. Does he change from the character we meet in the *Henry IV*s, or is his apparent transformation into the heroic talisman of England's glory days merely a development of characteristics of which we have had evidence throughout? One thing is for sure: he'd have made your Top Ten Favourite Actors of All Time.

Unfortunately, this has led (and leads) the play to be interpreted in a variety of ways: as a romantic celebration of the unification of England and France, through the ultimate coupling of a golden pair; as an ironic satire on the futility of war; as a hymn to a latter-day Greek god of heroism; xenophobic jingoism, subversive pacifism – you pays your money and you takes your choice. But because it is capable of having the subjective bias of its interpreters thrust upon it – almost more than any other play in the canon – it has yielded wildly swinging versions in performance and polarised views in print. A play 'which men of action have been wont silently to admire . . . and literary men volubly to condemn' (Dover Wilson).

Hazlitt begins it in 1817. Post Waterloo, filled with anger at the restoration of the Bourbons in France, he fired off a republican salvo at England's favourite play and its military hero. 'Henry because he did not know how to govern his own kingdom determined to make war upon his neighbours. Because his own title to the crown was doubtful he laid claim to that of France. Because he did not know how to exercise the enormous power which had just dropped into his hands to any one good purpose he immediately undertook (a cheap and obvious resource of sovereignty) to do all the mischief he could.'[1] The Irish Unionist Edward Dowden went into a paroxysm of orgasmic ecstasy over Henry as 'Shakespeare's ideal of manhood in the sphere of practical achievement':

Henry's freedom from egoism, his modesty, his integrity, his joyous humour, his practical piety, his habit of judging things by natural and not artificial standards all these are various developments of the central elements of his character, his noble realisation of fact.[2]

A closer examination of the text, however, reveals the play to be one of the best examples of Stephen Greenblatt's invisible bullet theory,[3] a play riddled with subversion but also one demonstrating Shakespeare's ability to bob and duck and dive and weave away from any suggestion that he is unpatriotic. Rather like Bertolt Brecht's defence during the McCarthy Communist witch-hunt of the '50s in America. Yet a modern reading of the play cannot fail to come down on the side of pacifism and see how a war of political expediency was won more by luck than judgement, and, historically, through the superior fire-power of the long bow – 'which every schoolboy know'. Bolingbroke's dying injunction 'to busy giddy minds with foreign quarrels' is here taken up in France with a vengeance.

Holinshed, the main source for the play, concludes with the following tribute to Henry:

This Henrie was a king, of life without spot, a prince whome all men loved, and of none disdained, a capteine against whome fortune never frowned, nor mischance once spurned, whose people him so severe a justicer both loved and obeid (and so humane withall) that he left no offence unpunished, nor freendship unrewarded; a terrour to rebels, and supressour of sedition, his virtues notable, his qualities most praiseworthy.[4]

The above has been taken by many to be the definitive judgement that history makes on Henry, but this is to ignore the small print further down. Here, there is a piece of Henry's bullshit on his death-bed, protesting the purity of his motives for invading France.

And herewith he protested unto them, that neither the ambitious desire to enlarge his dominions, neither to

purchase vain renowne and worldlie fame, nor anie other consideration had moved him to take the warrs in hand; but onelie that in prosecuting his just title, he might in the end attaine to a perfect peace, and come to enjoy those peeces of his inheritance, which to him of right belonged: and that before the beginning of the same warres, he was fullie persuaded by men both wise and of great holiness of life, that upon such intent he might and ought both begin the same warres, and follow them, till he have brought them to an end justlie and rightlie, and that without all danger of God's displeasure or perill of soul.

A more succinct description of Bush/Blair and their motives for invading Iraq cannot be found. And for WMD, in *Henry V* read Salic law.

Salic law is the tortuous route whereby the Church attempts to prove Henry's right to the throne of France through the female line. Holinshed describes the practice as 'sharp invention' and this is the line taken up by Shakespeare. We meet the Archbishop of Canterbury and the Bishop of Ely discussing a new law passed by the Commons, stripping the Church of a large part of its possessions and putting the proceeds to such ungodly uses as the relief of the poor, aged and sick. Oh, yes, and for Henry's own personal use. They work on Henry, who is not only 'a true lover of the Holy Church', but who has received from them massive support for his war chest for the war against France . They have given him

> ' . . . a greater sum
> Than ever at one time the clergy yet
> Did . . . part withal'
> (Act I.1)

– a massive bribe, in other words, to keep his hands off Church wealth, and deliberately egging him on to pursue those 'foreign quarrels'. (Note that Henry is not loth to follow his father's advice; a standing army is already in position for that war, without the need for an excuse to legitimise it. Salic law is the icing.)

The two bishops, working a pincer movement on Henry, sound

more like two conniving politicians indulging in a bit of brown envelope business than men of the cloth. Corruption never worse than when at the top. It was ever thus:

> CANTERBURY: My lord, I'll tell you. That self bill is urged
> Which in th'eleventh year of the last King's reign
> Was like, and had indeed against us passed,
> But that the scambling and unquiet time
> Did push it out of farther question.
>
> ELY: But how, my lord, shall we resist it now?
>
> CANTERBURY: It must be thought on. If it pass against us,
> We lose the better half of our possession;
> For all the temporal lands which men devout
> By testament have given to the Church
> Would they strip from us; being valued thus –
> As much as would maintain, to the King's honour,
> Full fifteen earls, and fifteen hundred knights,
> Six thousand and two hundred good esquires;
> And, to relief of lazars and weak age,
> Of indigent faint souls past corporal toil,
> A hundred almshouses right well supplied;
> And, to the coffers of the King beside,
> A thousand pounds by th'year. Thus runs the bill.
>
> ELY: This would drink deep.
>
> CANTERBURY: 'Twould drink the cup and all.
>
> ELY: But what prevention?

and

> ELY: But, my good lord,
> How now for mitigation of this bill
> Urged by the Commons? Doth his majesty

Incline to it, or no?

CANTERBURY: He seems indifferent,
Or rather swaying more upon our part
Than cherishing th'exhibiters against us;
For I have made an offer to his majesty –
Upon our spiritual Convocation,
And in regard of causes now in hand,
Which I have opened to his grace at large
As touching France – to give a greater sum
Than ever at one time the clergy yet
Did to his predecessors part withal.
(Act I.1)

It is to deflect this Bill, then, that the boys vigorously persuade Henry of his claim to the French crown. And thus begins the long-winded, convoluted, pedantic explanation of the family tree that proves his lineage. A taste:

CANTERBURY: . . . King Pepin, which deposèd Childeric,
Did, as heir general, being descended
Of Blithild, which was daughter to King Clothair,
Make claim and title to the crown of France.
Hugh Capet also – who usurped the crown
Of Charles the Duke of Lorraine, sole heir male
Of the true line and stock of Charles the Great –
To find his title with some shows of truth,
Though in pure truth it was corrupt and naught,
Conveyed himself as th'heir to th'Lady Lingare,
Daughter to Charlemain, who was the son
To Lewis the Emperor, and Lewis the son
Of Charles the Great. Also King Lewis the Tenth,
Who was sole heir to the usurper Capet,
Could not keep quiet in his conscience,
Wearing the crown of France, till satisfied
That fair Queen Isabel, his grandmother,
Was lineal of the Lady Ermengare,

Daughter to Charles the foresaid Duke of Lorraine . . .
(Act I.2)

And so on and so on, finishing with a line that, whichever it is played, is bound to get a laugh:

So that, as clear as is the summer's sun,
(pause for laughter to subside)
King Pepin's title, and Hugh Capet's claim,
King Lewis his satisfaction, all appear
To hold in right and title of the female . . .

Amidst all this we mustn't lose sight of the fact that what is on offer here is a dossier of dodgy proof providing a trumped-up excuse to invade France. Familiar or what? The wish is always father to the deed where extension of wealth and power are concerned. Despite the Duke of Exeter, Henry's uncle, asserting to the French king that the claim has not been 'picked from the wormholes of long vanished days', it is strange to say the least that nobody has ever mentioned this spurious claim before, so it can hardly have been a cornerstone of English foreign policy. And where have we heard *that* before?

. . . That you may know
'Tis no sinister nor no awkward claim
Picked from the worm-holes of long-vanished days,
Nor from the dust of old oblivion raked,
He sends you this most memorable line,
In every branch truly demonstrative,
Willing you overlook this pedigree;
And when you find him evenly derived
From his most famed of famous ancestors,
Edward the Third, he bids you then resign
Your crown and kingdom, indirectly held
From him, the native and true challenger.
(Act II.4)

Egged on by the clergy, who would rather see him destroy France than lose any of their land and possessions, Henry buys this load of political bollocks proving his hereditary right through the female line. The claim is ruthlessly prosecuted and the demand to hand over his throne is put to the French king with an army already in France. Henry was clearly predetermined to invade and uses the Salic law merely as a pretext. With God on his side who can blame him? 'May I with right with conscience make this claim?' says Henry and the Archbishop of Canterbury replies, 'The sin upon my head, dread sovereign!' It bothered Henry not a jot that his own claim to the throne, achieved only by the deposition of Richard II by his father Henry Bolingbroke, was illegitimate and that in England the female line was debarred from inheriting. No. 'Salic law', the equivalent of UN Resolution 43, legitimised the war. God has said there are WMD, so WMD we will find. And France? Like Iraq, no joy, only devastation:

> BURGUNDY: . . . let it not disgrace me
> If I demand, before this royal view,
> What rub or what impediment there is
> Why that the naked, poor, and mangled peace,
> Dear nurse of arts, plenties, and joyful births,
> Should not in this best garden of the world,
> Our fertile France, put up her lovely visage?
> Alas, she hath from France too long been chased,
> And all her husbandry doth lie on heaps,
> Corrupting in it own fertility.
> Her vine, the merry cheerer of the heart,
> Unprunèd dies; her hedges even-pleached,
> Like prisoners wildly overgrown with hair,
> Put forth disordered twigs; her fallow leas
> The darnel, hemlock, and rank fumitory
> Doth root upon, while that the coulter rusts
> That should deracinate such savagery.
> The even mead, that erst brought sweetly forth
> The freckled cowslip, burnet and green clover,
> Wanting the scythe, all uncorrected, rank,
> Conceives by idleness, and nothing teems
> But hateful docks, rough thistles, kecksies, burs,

Losing both beauty and utility;
And as our vineyards, fallows, meads, and hedges,
Defective in their natures, grow to wildness,
Even so our houses and ourselves and children
Have lost, or do not learn for want of time,
The sciences that should become our country,
But grow like savages – as soldiers will
That nothing do but meditate on blood –
To swearing and stern looks, diffused attire,
And everything that seems unnatural.
(Act V.2)

The disordered garden in *Richard II* has now become a picture painted by Burgundy of devastation covering the land and the people. Henry has put the garden of England in order and, with the arrests of the traitors Scroop, Grey and Cambridge at Southampton, given it some judicious pruning. But in so doing he has ruined the garden of France. Burgundy's sober speech casts a cloud over the English victory celebrations, reminding us that Henry's war has decimated a land, a people and its culture. Shades again of Iraq.

* * *

Henry is ruthless in eliminating any who get in his way. The treachery of the conspirators Cambridge, Scrope and Grey came to light on the night before Henry's departure for Calais, yet Shakespeare begins his scene, Act II.2, by suggesting that their treachery is clear long before this moment:

BEDFORD: For God his grace is bold to trust these traitors.

EXETER: They shall be apprehended by and by.

The plan is already in place to trap them with an admission of their guilt. The treachery of the conspirators consists, according to Exeter, simply of the intention to murder Henry for foreign cash. A contract killing set up by France. Henry, obviously well informed of this, his intelligence system working well, tricks the conspirators into signing their own death warrants. They confess that their motive was greed; but one of them, Richard Earl of Cambridge, hints at a deeper motive:

> **For me the gold of France did not seduce,**
> **Although I did admit it as a motive**
> **The sooner to affect what I intended.**

The three traitors, Richard Plantagenet, Henry Scrope and Sir Thomas Grey, actually represent, as Shakespeare well knew, the cause of the deposed Richard II. This is one of those moments where Shakespeare hints darkly at a sub-text, a hidden bullet leaving us to consider its impact. Henry has succeeded in boiling down all political problems to a question of loyalty. If Englishmen are not wholeheartedly with Henry, they are against him – and that means complicity with France. The idea of a totalitarian state completely purged of all internal opposition, all dissent suppressed and complete loyalty guaranteed, is an illusion, perpetrated by a leader determined to leave his mark on history as the perfect ruler. Blair was obviously carrying his copy of *Henry V* around in his back pocket when he steamrollered over the dissident voices of Cook, Galloway and the chorus of disapproval.

The ruthlessness shown domestically is but a taste of the chilling pragmatism shown in war. Though Holinshed describes the atrocities that actually took place at the siege of Harfleur, Shakespeare is content merely to let Henry utter the threat of violence, leaving us in no doubt through the graphic detail, that he would have no compunction at all in letting loose his dogs of war on the citizens of Harfleur if it became necessary. He says to the Mayor,

> **If I begin the battery once again,**
> **I will not leave the half-achievèd Harfleur**
> **Till in her ashes she lie burièd.**
> **. . . Therefore, you men of Harfleur,**
> **Take pity of your town and of your people**
> **Whiles yet my solders are in my command . . .**
> **If not, why, in a moment look to see**
> **The blind and bloody soldier with foul hand**
> **Defile the locks of your shrill-shrieking daughters;**

Your fathers taken by the silver beards,
And their most reverend heads dashed to the walls;
Your naked infants spitted upon pikes,
Whiles the mad mothers with their howls confused
Do break the clouds, as did the wives of Jewry
At Herod's bloody-hunting slaughtermen.
(Act III.3)

This is the streak of ruthlessness, witnessed at the banishment of Falstaff, which now finds its apotheosis in this war with France. Bardolph, his erstwhile servant and supposed friend, is summarily executed without a backward glance. A terse injunction 'to kill all the prisoners', flying in the face of combat procedure, is a pragmatic decision taken in the face of possible defeat. Down in numbers? Release those soldiers whose duty it is to guard the prisoners in order to have more in the front line. Consequence? Too bad – the prisoners must die. In retaliation, the French kill the boys guarding the luggage. 'I was not angry till I came to France/Until this instant' says Henry. 'Kill all the boys and the luggage? It's expressly against the law of arms!' says Fluellen (Act IV.7) Not a word about killing prisoners being against the law of arms. Not only that, but Gower attributes Henry's act to revenge for the above and that it is therefore just. This ignores the fact that the order to kill the prisoners was given before the action of the French. 'Wherefore the king most worthily hath ordered every soldier to cut his prisoner's throat. O, 'tis a gallant king!'

This gallant, Welsh king does not even know that he has won the battle and has to be told by the French envoy, Mountjoy (Act IV.7). When informed that some ten thousand French had died and only twenty nine English, he reads out the names of four noblemen and says, 'None else of name; and of all other men/But five and twenty' (Act IV.8). Presumably, these were commoners and not worthy of being read out. He does not even bother to see if Court and Bates, with whom he had personal contact the night before, are on the list. (We know the exact numbers and names of British and American dead in Iraq, but Iraqis? 10,000? 150,000? Who cares.) 'O God, thy arm was here!/And not to us but to thy arm alone' – or rather the arms of the Welsh archers. It's a good job God was somewhere. He certainly wasn't with the French. Or the Iraqis. 'We few, we happy few, we band of brothers . . . '

* * *

The ironic and subversive is most evident in the Chorus. After apologising to us for not having hydraulics at his disposal, thus preparing us for the massive suspension of disbelief as epic words are matched by puny action, he proceeds to pull the wool over our eyes as Henry pulls it over others'. This has the effect of working on us as a kind of Brechtian alienation device, set the coconuts up to knock 'em down. The German poet, Heinrich Heine destroyed the Romantic Movement in Germany with 'Stimmungsbrechung' (1797-1856) – breaking the mood. He would finish a cloying description of a sunset with a line akin to 'and suddenly a feeling of nausea swept over me like a cup of cold sick'. The Chorus is a bit like that. Nothing is said that can be taken at face value. 'Now all the youth of England are on fire and silken dalliance in the wardrobe lies' (Act II.1). Who are these lads, these hearts, these 'culled and choice-drawn cavaliers'? None other than Pistol, Nym and Bardolph, whose mission is to go to France . . . 'like horse leeches my boys/to suck to suck the very blood to suck!' (Act II.3). (In the very next scene, the French king remarks, 'Thus come the English upon us', creating an umbilical cord of irony between British imperialism and football hooligans.) And what are their exploits? Do we see brave heroics matching the Chorus's high-flown rhetoric of great deeds? No. We see them hiding from the action, being pistol-whipped into battle and the only deeds are those of theft, pillage and desecration; the stealing of crucifixes and fire shovels. The glory of the Battle of Agincourt? We see none of it. Only the decidedly unglamorous sight of Pistol kicking the shit out of a wounded Frenchman and bribed to hang on to him illegally instead of turning him over.

The Choruses claim that the French 'Shake in their fear and with pale policy/Seek to divert the English purposes.', (Act II.Chorus), is obviously meant to prepare us for an easy victory. Far from quaking in their shoes, the French are making intelligent military preparation and indulging in over-confident boasting about the rival merits of their horses. The Chorus's announcements of what happens next are often at odds with the events. He leaves us totally unprepared for the first bishop scene, the first Eastcheap scene and the leek-eating scene, all of which come immediately after he has told us that the action is somewhere else. All this is an argument for re-ordering certain of the Chorus's passages to coincide with the action, though I have yet to find an editor with the temerity to do so. Leave that to insouciant directors. Or maybe Shakespeare was being deliberate in spreading structural confusion.

'A little touch of Harry in the night?'

> **. . . O now, who will behold**
> **The royal Captain of this ruined band**
> **Walking from watch to watch, from tent to tent,**
> **Let him cry, 'Praise and glory on his head!'**
> **For forth he goes and visits all his host,**
> **Bids them good morrow with a modest smile,**
> **And calls them brothers, friends, and countrymen.**
> **Upon his royal face there is no note**
> **How dread an army hath enrounded him,**
> **Nor doth he dedicate one jot of colour**
> **Unto the weary and all-watchèd night,**
> **But freshly looks, and overbears attaint**
> **With cheerful semblance and sweet majesty;**
> **That every wretch, pining and pale before,**
> **Beholding him, plucks comfort from his looks.**
> **A largess universal, like the sun,**
> **His liberal eye doth give to every one,**
> **Thawing cold fear, that mean and gentle all**
> **Behold, as may unworthiness define,**
> **A little touch of Harry in the night.**
> **(Chorus IV)**

Oh yes? We see none of this. Borrowing Sir Thomas Erpingham's cloak under the pretext of wishing solitude, Henry disguises himself and walks about the tents, on the eve of the Battle of Agincourt, eavesdropping to hear what is being said about him – the Welsh paranoia – (cf. *Richard III* on the eve of the Battle of Bosworth). Far from geeing up the troops with some comforting words, Henry gets into an argument with his soldiers about the justness of his cause, his frustration boiling over into petulance at his inability to reveal his true identity, and conceiving a vengeful plan to get his own back one day in his true persona.

This is the scene (Act IV. 1) on which the central pacifist argument of the play rests. He falls into conversation with three soldiers – Bates, Court and Williams, shivering in the trenches, waiting for the dawn to rise that will herald the attack. The king's army is already on retreat, having suffered heavy losses and riddled with dysentery. Williams unknowlingly engages the king in an argument on the nature of war, equality and the unbridgeable gap between subject and king. When is a war just? What's the king think of it all? The scene confounds all the jingoism associated with the play and puts the case for pacifism, humanity and democratic involvement in the consequences of decisions taken by leaders. Secure in his disguise (and his Welsh accent), Henry attempts to place the king on the same footing as these, his common soldiers. 'I think the king is but a man, as I am'. Bates is having none of it; he quickly gets under Henry's skin (would Henry's assumed accent slip under pressure?) *This* is how an ordinary man who is not a member of any aristocratic *elite* feels on the night before a battle.

BATES: He may show what outward courage he will, but I believe, as cold a night as 'tis, he could wish himself in Thames up to the neck; and so I would he were, and I by him, at all adventures, so we were quit here.

KING HENRY: By my troth, I will speak my conscience of the King: I think he would not wish himself anywhere but where he is.

BATES: Then I would he were here alone; so should he be sure to be ransomed, and a many poor men's lives saved.

KING HENRY: I dare say you love him not so ill to wish him here alone, howsoever you speak this to feel other men's minds. Methinks I could not die anywhere so contented as in

> **the King's company, his cause being just and his quarrel honourable.**
>
> **WILLIAMS: That's more than we know.**
>
> **BATES: Ay, or more than we should seek after; for we know enough if we know we are the King's subjects. If his cause be wrong, our obedience to the King wipes the crime of it out of us.**

Bates challenging Henry's motives for prosecuting the war in the first place questions the whole moral justice of the king's expedition and the dubious political gain from a victory over France. The whole *raison d'être* is examined in the light of the blind obedience demanded of a compliant and willing fighting force, suggesting that, in an ideal democratic world, the people would have a say in whether they are going to give their lives to a dubious cause or not, and that kings (or Prime Ministers) should fight their own battles if they are so keen.

Williams continues the debate, placing Henry in the morally indefensible position of being responsible for death and injury, and for creating cripples, orphans and widows in pursuit of a selfish, unjust cause.

> **But if the cause be not good, the King himself hath a heavy reckoning to make, when all those legs, and arms, and heads, chopped off in a battle, shall join together at the latter day, and cry all, 'We died at such a place'; some swearing, some crying for a surgeon, some upon their wives left poor behind them, some upon the debts they owe, some upon their children rawly left. I am afeard there are few die well that die in a battle, for how can they charitably dispose of anything when blood is their argument? Now, if these men do not die well, it will be a black matter for the King that led them to it, who to disobey were against all proportion of subjection.**

This is one of Shakespeare's most cogent arguments against the megalomaniac ambition of war-mongering tyrants sacrificing thousands of lives (millions) in pursuit of the territorial imperative. Williams insists that all the responsibility for the carnage of the war finally is the king's. Henry is completely wrong-footed, ducking out characteristically of the moral responsibility for his actions and his people, invoking duty to God and country as his principal argument. Williams in no way buys this, recognising the argument for what it is, a cop out. Henry finds himself backed into a corner at Williams's insistence that there is an unbridgeable gap of such inequality between subject and king that the abuse of that power is what has led to the situation in which they now find themselves. The argument is unanswerable and, petulantly, Henry seeks a way out that only serves to reinforce Williams's analysis of the essential difference between them. He picks a quarrel knowing that at some time in the future he will assert his authority over Williams in the only way he knows how – the imperial power of king over subject. Thou shalt obey.

WILLIAMS: 'Tis certain, every man that dies ill, the ill upon his own head – the King is not to answer it.

BATES: I do not desire he should answer for me, and yet I determine to fight lustily for him.

KING HENRY: I myself heard the King say he would not be ransomed.

WILLIAMS: Ay, he said so, to make us fight cheerfully: but when our throats are cut he may be ransomed, and we ne'er the wiser.

KING HENRY: If I live to see it, I will never trust his word after.

WILLIAMS: You pay him then! That's a perilous shot out of an elder-gun, that a poor and private displeasure can do against a monarch! You may as well go about to turn the sun to ice, with fanning in his face with a peacock's feather. You'll never trust his word after! Come, 'tis a foolish saying.

KING HENRY: Your reproof is something too round. I should be angry with you, if the time were convenient.

WILLIAMS: Let it be a quarrel between us, if you live.

KING HENRY: I embrace it.

WILLIAMS: How shall I know thee again?

KING HENRY: Give me any gage of thine, and I will wear it in my bonnet: then, if ever thou dar'st acknowledge it, I will make it my quarrel.

The question of responsibility touches a raw nerve in Henry throughout the play. The blame always falls elsewhere: on the Church for encouraging him to go to war; on the Dauphin for sending him tennis balls; on the French king for resisting his claim; to the citizens of Harfleur for having the temerity to defend their town (Act I.2 ll 18-28; Act I.2 ll 282-284; Act II.4 ll 105-109; Act III.3 ll 1-43). After the departure of the three soldiers, Henry is able to return, in soliloquy, to his royal identity and release his frustration (thank goodness he can now drop that accent). It's all so unfair! Kingship carries with it a heavy burden of responsibility:

Upon the King! Let us our lives, our souls,
Our debts, our careful wives,
Our children, and our sins, lay on the King!
We must bear all. O hard condition,
Twin-born with greatness, subject to the breath
Of every fool, whose sense no more can feel
But his own wringing! What infinite heart's ease
Must kings neglect that private men enjoy!
(Act IV.1)

In the aftermath of the dispute, Henry reveals his true self, his contempt for the ordinary class, something we have been aware of from his early posturing days in The Boar's Head Tavern. The king's subjects are described by terms of aristocratic contempt – 'fool . . . wretch . . . slave . . . peasant':

And but for ceremony, such a wretch,

> Winding up days with toil, and nights with sleep,
> Had the fore-hand and vantage of a king.
> The slave, a member of the country's peace,
> Enjoys it, but in gross brain little wots [knows]
> What watch the king keeps to maintain the peace,
> Whose hours the peasant best advantages.
> (Act IV.1)

His reference to Williams as a fool with a gross brain is bitter and unfair and his anger unreasonable and unjust. However, significantly at no time does he say that Williams is wrong, the worm of conscience gnawing at him as he wriggles on the hook.

So what are we to make of the methods of this 'star of England'? That he carries the guilt around with him of his father's usurpation is palpably obvious. Before Agincourt he prays:

> KING HENRY: . . . Not today, O Lord,
> O not today, think not upon the fault
> My father made in compassing the crown!
> I Richard's body have interrèd new,
> And on it have bestowed more contrite tears
> Than from it issued forcèd drops of blood.
> Five hundred poor I have in yearly pay,
> Who twice a day their withered hands hold up
> Toward heaven, to pardon blood; and I have built
> Two chantries where the sad and solemn priests
> Sing still for Richard's soul. More will I do,
> Though all that I can do is nothing worth,
> Since that my penitence comes after all,
> Imploring pardon.

He is paying five hundred extras a yearly sum to pray twice a day for his soul! And he's got a bunch of priests in two specially-built chantries singing to get him into Heaven. That's real abuse of the public purse – beats Charlie's helicopter any day.

* * *

'Il faut que j'apprenne a parler'.[5] It is necessary that I learn English. Katherine does not have to learn English because she is a willing participant in a love match. No. It is the *'il faut'* that gives the game away. It is an imperative. There is compulsion. Unfortunately, if I am going to be given away against my wishes, then I've got to get my head round those awful flat vowel sounds.

Kate is Henry's 'capital demand'. She is goods, chattels. It is necessary that he conquer Katherine as he conquers France. His male pride demands it. And the moment that we see him win both is the moment that he plants a kiss on her lips (Act V.2). We have been conditioned, particularly as a result of the Oliver and Branagh films, to believe that Henry's winning of Katherine is a love scene in which two stars of their respective countries become the Burton and Taylor, the Posh and Becks, of the Anglo-French alliance. The truth is that the wooing is a whirlwind five-minute job, while the rest of the court stand outside the door waiting for Henry to get a result:

> **I am glad thou canst speak no better English; for if thou couldst, thou wouldst find me such a plain King that thou wouldst think I had sold my farm to buy my crown. I know no ways to mince it in love, but directly to say, 'I love you': then if you urge me farther than to say, 'Do you, in faith?' I wear out my suit. Give me your answer, i'faith, do; and so clap hands, and a bargain. How say you, lady?**
> **(Act V.2)**

It is a scene between an arrogant showman and a recalcitrant young girl who knows there can be only one ending but is determined to put up a fight. Five minutes. Henry pulls out all the stops, tries every trick. It would seem that he has learnt his wooing technique at Hotspur's knee for there is more than the blunt, plain-peaking persona of Harry Percy in the way he protests his simplicity, honesty, lack of affectation, inability to dance, rhyme, play a musical instrument and above all pleading an almost dyslexic inarticulacy:

> **KING HENRY: Marry, if you would put me to verses, or to dance for your sake, Kate, why, you undid me. For the one, I**

have neither words nor measure; and for the other, I have no strength in measure, yet a reasonable measure in strength. If I could win a lady at leapfrog, or by vaulting into my saddle with my armour on my back, under the correction of bragging be it spoken, I should quickly leap into a wife. Or if I might buffet for my love, or bound my horse for her favours, I could lay on like a butcher, and sit like a jackanapes, never off. But, before God, Kate, I cannot look greenly, nor gasp out my eloquence, nor I have no cunning in protestation: only downright oaths, which I never use till urged, nor never break for urging.

(Act V.2)

Liar. From the moment we first meet Henry we have been aware of Hal/Henry's power of oratory and persuasion. Has he forgotten the breach? St Crispin's Day? Henry the actor. The protestations of plain soldier don't cut it when set against the arrogance which he displays in his treatment of his erstwhile companions and in the aftermath of the argument with Bates, Court and Williams. His appellation and constant repetition of 'Kate' for 'Katherine' has the bluntness of Hotspur about it – an attempt to be down-to-earth and matey. I'm 'enry V, but you can call me 'al. Even in his disguised encounter with Pistol in the trenches he calls himself Harry Le Roy, banking on Pistol's ignorance of French not to know that *roi* is king.

If thou canst love a fellow of this temper, Kate, whose face is not worth sunburning, that never looks in his glass for love of anything he sees there, let thine eye be thy cook. I speak to thee plain soldier. If thou canst love me for this, take me; if not, to say to thee that I shall die is true – but for thy love, by the Lord, no – yet I love thee too. And while thou liv'st, dear Kate, take a fellow of plain and uncoined constancy; for he perforce must do thee right, because he hath not the gift to woo in other places. For these fellows of infinite tongue, that can rhyme themselves into ladies' favours, they do always reason themselves out again. What! A speaker is but a prater, a rhyme is but a ballad. A good leg will fall; a straight back will stoop; a black beard will turn white; a curled pate will grow bald; a fair face will wither; a full eye will wax hollow: but a good heart, Kate, is the sun and the moon – or rather, the sun, and not the moon; for it shines bright and never changes, but keeps his course truly. If thou would have such a one, take me; and take me, take a soldier; take a soldier, take a king. And what say'st thou then to my love? Speak, my fair, and fairly, I pray thee.

Henry's true motives become apparent in the very next speech:

KATHERINE: Is it possible dat I sould love de *ennemi* of *France*?

HENRY: No, it is not possible you should love the enemy of France, Kate; but in loving me you should love the friend of France, for I love France so well that I will not part with a village of it – I will have it all mine: and Kate, when France is mine, and I am yours, then yours is France, and you are mine.

I love France so well that I will not part with a village of it. Thus *la belle France* and the *belle* Katherine are synonymous. One is the other, love of land conquers all. Henry's dream of reviving the Crusade, another inheritance from his father, produces the sharpest irony of all:

Shall not thou and I, between Saint Dennis and Saint George, compound a boy, half French half English, that shall go to Constantinople and take the Turk by the beard?

Note that Henry does not offer to go on a crusade himself, offering up a putative future son in his place. But the boy they compounded was Henry VI, the coupling producing a child who will preside over disaster.

* * *

At the siege of Harfleur, the Welsh and the Irish touch on the raw nerve of national identity:

> **FLUELLEN: Captain Macmorris, I think, look you, under your correction, there is not many of your nation –**
>
> **MACMORRIS: Of my nation? What ish my nation? Ish a villain, and a bastard, and a knave, and a rascal. What ish my nation? Who talks of my nation?**
>
> (Act III.2)

Before the projected row over Celtic identity can flare into full-scale physical aggression, 'the town sounds a parley'. English, Scots, Welsh, Irish are united once again in their desire to defeat the enemy across the water.

The question of nationhood is still with us, devolution in Scotland and Wales having raised as many problems as it has solved. The fact that the argument between Fluellen and Macmorris takes place during the heat of battle says much about the passion with which the Celts believe in an identity separate from that of the Anglo Saxon. The dispute today is carried on at both a political and a sporting level and, though of recent years an interloper, Italy, has come along to play with the ball, the heart of the yearly rugby fest in the Northern hemisphere is still the hundred years-old Five Nations tournament. It wasn't always so. This strange game with barbaric rules of engagement where big men grunt and groan and fight and push as they grab and grapple with each other, more often than not incurring black eyes, broken noses and bloody wounds from the studs of a stamping boot, was played as a 'friendly' tournament between the four nations of the UK. Then a fifth was admitted, a foreigner whose roads were cobbled and whose loos were holes in the ground. How on earth did they manage to cook so well in such circumstances? And this nation played a rugby that was as far from the biff and bash of this septic isle as is pole dancing from ballet. France was, as ever, the one to beat.

The ground has shifted, though, over the years, and Scotland, Ireland and Wales are united in their hunger to beat England and rejoice at a French win over the 'auld enemy'. The dispute is over a piece of leather whose shape defies all logic, an apt metaphor for what outsiders are unable to perceive as a problem, but which at home manifests itself in vast cultural differences of language, temperament and culture. What is my nation indeed? Shakespeare puts together an almost microcosmic, stereotypical group of representatives – a voluble philosophising Welshman, an aggressive Irishman with a short fuse, literally – his solution to ending the siege of Harfleur is to dynamite the lot – 'By my hand . . . the work ish ill done . . . I would have blowed up the town, so Chrish save me, la! In an hour. O, 'tish ill done, 'tish ill done!'.

> **FLUELLEN: Look you, if you take the matter otherwise than is meant, Captain Macmorris, peradventure I shall think you do not use me with that affability as in discretion you ought to use me, look you, being as good a man as yourself, both in the disciplines of war, and in the derivation of my birth, and in other particularities.**

> **MACMORRIS: I do not know you so good a man as myself. So Chrish save me, I will cut off your head.**
> **(Act III.2)**

Here, the Englishman Captain Gower is the appeaser: 'Gentlemen both, you will mistake each other'. Fight the French rather than fight with each other.

What was it that Shakespeare spotted that made him prefigure the modern stereotype of the Irish as hard-drinking, bomb-toting and spoiling for a fight? In this scenario the quarrel is between the Welsh and the Irish, something that today only takes the form of friendly rivalry, a mutual appreciation of each other's culture uniting them rather than separating. After all, Cardiff is closer to Dublin than it is to London as the crow flies, give or take the Irish Sea in between, and the coast of Ireland can be seen from parts of Wales. The landscape of Ceredigion (Cardigan) merges seamlessly with that of Wicklow and as for the Highlands of Scotland, they are further from Westminster than is the coast of France. Is it any wonder that the resentment of hundreds of years of oppressive English rule still survives, not just under the surface but boils over into acts of violence? This dispute over nationhood will run and run until the North of Ireland is united with the South, the West Lothian question is settled in Scotland and the Welsh Assembly has devolved powers to match those of Edinburgh.

* * *

For a play that has traditionally come to embody the great and glorious feats of English imperialism there are an awful lot of Welsh about. And more than any other play, with the exception of the Mortimer/Glendower/Lady Mortimer episode in *Henry IV, Part 1* (see the *Henry IV*s), *Henry V* reveals Shakespeare's appreciation of the people and culture of that small country, Wales. Not only does the character of the voluble Fluellen run right through the play, but his English companion, Captain Gower, has a Welsh name, as does Henry's protagonist, Williams. But the most interesting aspect of the Welshness of the play is Henry's insistence himself on his Welsh credentials:

FLUELLEN: Your grandfather of famous memory, an't please your majesty, and your great-uncle Edward the Black Prince of Wales, as I have read in the chronicles, fought a most prave pattle here in France.

KING HENRY: They did, Fluellen.

FLUELLEN: Your majesty says very true. If your majesties is remember of it, the Welshmen did good service in a garden where leeks did grow, wearing leeks in their Monmouth caps, which your majesty know to this hour is an honourable badge of the service; and I do believe your majesty takes no scorn to wear the leek upon Saint Tavy's day.

**KING HENRY: I wear it for a memorable honour;
For I am Welsh, you know, good countryman.**

FLUELLEN: All the water in Wye cannot wash your

109

majesty's Welsh plood out of your pody, I can tell you that. God pless it and preserve it, as long as it pleases His grace, and His majesty too!

KING HENRY: Thanks, good my countryman.

FLUELLEN: By Jeshu, I am your majesty's countryman, I care not who know it; I will confess it to all the 'orld. I need not to be ashamed of your majesty, praised be God, so long as your majesty is an honest man.

KING HENRY: God keep me so!
(Act IV.7)

On the prowl round the camp on the eve of the Battle of Agincourt he encounters Pistol:

PISTOL: The King's a bawcock, and a heart of gold,
A lad of life, an imp of fame;
Of parents good, of fist most valiant.
I kiss his dirty shoe, and from heartstring
I love the lovely bully. What is thy name?

KING HENRY: Harry le Roy.

PISTOL: Le Roy? A Cornish name. Art thou of Cornish crew?

KING HENRY: No, I am a Welshman.

PISTOL: Know'st thou Fluellen?

KING HENRY: Yes.

PISTOL: Tell him I'll knock his leek about his pate
Upon Saint Davy's day.

KING HENRY: Do not you wear your dagger in your cap that

day, lest he knock that about yours.

PISTOL: Art thou his friend?

KING HENRY: And his kinsman too.

PISTOL: The *figo* for thee then!

KING HENRY: I thank you. God be with you!
(Act IV.1)

Welsh and proud of it. *En route* to the confrontation with Williams, Bates and Court, he overhears a conversation with the passing Fluellen and Gower:

KING HENRY: Though it appear a little out of fashion,
There is much care and valour in this Welshman.

Sympathy with a fellow Welshman. And it is for Fluellen that Shakespeare reserves the most cogent statement of his appreciation of Welsh culture. Earlier, the yob Pistol has sneered at Fluellen and derided his nationality. The Battle of Agincourt is over but the Battle of the Leek is about to begin.

FLUELLEN: . . . You called me yesterday mountain-squire, but I will make you today a squire of low degree. I pray you fall to – if you can mock a leek, you can eat a leek.

GOWER: Enough, Captain you have astonished him.

FLUELLEN: I say, I will make him eat some part of my leek, or I will peat his pate four days. Bite, I pray you, it is good for your green wound and your ploody coxcomb.

PISTOL: Must I bite?

FLUELLEN: Yes, certainly; and out of doubt, and out of question too, and ambiguities.

PISTOL: By this leek, I will most horribly revenge – I eat and eat, I swear –

FLUELLEN: Eat, I pray you; will you have some more sauce to you leek? There is not enough leek to swear by.

PISTOL: Quiet thy cudgel, thou dost see I eat.

FLUELLEN: Much good do you, scauld knave, heartily. Nay, pray you throw none away, the skin is good for your broken coxcomb. When you take occasions to see leeks hereafter, I pray you mock at 'em, that is all.

PISTOL: Good!

FLUELLEN: Ay, leeks is good. Hold you, there is a groat to heal your pate.

PISTOL: Me a groat?

FLUELLEN: Yes, verily and in truth you shall take it, or I have another leek in my pocket which you shall eat.
(Act V.1)

And he produces a leek of Max Boycean proportions. However, it is left to the Englishman, Gower, to put the cultural boot in with a powerful plea for racial tolerance that goes beyond the local:

GOWER: Go, go, you are a counterfeit cowardly knave. Will you mock at an ancient tradition, begun upon an honourable respect, and worn as a memorable trophy of predeceased valour, and dare not avouch in your deeds any of your words? I have seen you gleeking and galling at this gentleman twice or thrice. You thought, because he could not speak English in the native garb, he could not therefore handle an English cudgel. You find it otherwise, and henceforth let a Welsh correction teach you a good English

condition. Fare ye well.
(Act V.1)

Apart from the odd excursion into French, German, Scots and Irish accents, nowhere else in Shakespeare do we find characters who consistently speak in the vernacular. Pastor Hugh Evans in *The Merry Wives of Windsor* and Fluellen, probably played by the same actor, both hold their style of language throughout the plays. It is strange that the compassion and understanding with which Shakespeare treated the Welsh has been consistently ignored by academics and critics alike. From a high point of respect during the reign of the Tudors, the prejudice gathered pace through the industrial revolution and has refused to go away. A language that was described by Shakespeare as 'that pretty Welsh' and 'as sweet as ditties penned, sung by a fair queen in a summers bower' was until recently suppressed and despised. No wonder the Welsh feel a constant need to affirm their identity. Where did Shakespeare get his knowledge of the Welsh? Certainly, the Welsh were held in high respect in the Tudor court, signifying a sea change in the attitude to what many had previously perceived as a barbaric land of mist and mountain. Did it come from his Welsh school master, Thomas Jenkins, at Stratford Upon Avon Grammar School? Or perhaps he learned the songs, myths and legends at the knee of his grandmother, Alys Griffin, a supposed descendant of the high kings of Wales. That would make Shakespeare Welsh . . .

Notes

1. Hazlitt, *Characters of Shakespeare's plays.*

2. Edward Dowden, *Shakespeare: A Critical Study of His Mind and Art.* A course of lectures at Trinity College, Dublin, 1875.

3. *Political Shakespeare,* ed Jonathon Dolimore and Alan Sinfield, MUP, 1985.

4. Holinshed, *Chronicles of England, Scotland and Ireland.*

5. In 1995 I was making a documentary in Ladywood, Birmingham, England, entitled *Shakespeare on the Estate* and I persuaded a duo drag act whom I met in a laundrette to perform the Katherine/Alice scene (III.4) at a ladies' hen night in the back room of a pub. Alice teaches Katherine the parts of the body which Katherine attempts to memorise, going back to the beginning each time adding a new one and ending with the bawdy mispronunciations of 'le foot et le count'. The crowd cottoned on and began to enumerate the body parts with the performers, ending with a triumphant shout of 'le fuck et le cunt'. It was clear that the scene is so structured as to invite the participation from the pit in a manner that the reading of the text does not reveal, nor have I seen explored in any contemporary production. Something that The Globe, with its middle class pass at audience involvement would do well to take on board.

The Henry VIs

A rose by any other name would smell . . .

The *Henry VI*s sprawl and brawl and run wildly up and down the field like a kid with a new pair of football boots that are too big. Tackling here, mis-kicking there, falling in the mud, skewing the ball out of play, diving headers and occasional flashes of brilliant ball control, dribbling past five defenders to plant the ball high in the top left-hand corner of the net. The physical metaphor is particularly apt, for in *Part 1* there are more than twenty-odd fights and on the diminutive stage of The Rose that would have been some feat. And we're not talking here of some slo-mo stylisation or pat-a-cake thrust and parry. We're talking real sword play, with real swords that would have enthused the lads and that the half-time pundits would have taken apart. I was once sitting in the front row of a performance of *King John* in a small theatre in Shibuya in Tokyo. As is the Japanese wont, they had placed the theatre on the twenty-third floor of a department building. The stage was the size of a pocket handkerchief but the cast numbered about thirty. At one point suddenly all thirty of them erupted onto stage and beat the shit out of each other – and I really mean the shit. Japanese actors fight for real. It was terrifying. I cowered in my seat. It must have been a bit like that at The Rose.

'But this lumbering shapeless chronicle begins to make sense if we can see it as being framed by the death of a hero and the birth of a monster'.[1] Whatever technical and linguistic shortcomings there may be in the plays, the *Henry VI*s cemented Shakespeare's reputation as the coming dramatist of the Elizabethan stage, drawing jealous fire from his contemporaries Ben Jonson and Robert Greene – the latter calling him an 'upstart crow[2], beautified with our feathers' in the belief that Shakespeare had filched material from his play. They had reason to be jealous. The crowds loved these swashbuckling adventures, taking familiar historical figures, turning them inside out and stabbing them in the back – Elizabethan spaghetti westerns.

The overwhelming effect of these plays, despite their unevenness, is a vision of Man the political animal manipulating events and bending fear and superstition to the demands of his ambition. He is simultaneously the perpetrator and victim of his own *real politik* – an existential force that recognises the absurdity of any belief other than in oneself.

In *Part 1* the decline of Britain in the 15th century mirrors that of the 20th – the loss of influence as an international power, and the deterioration of the domestic situation at home; and in both instances, wars are to blame. Division and internal weakness erodes and corrupts government. The last fifty years have seen the collapse of Britain as a real international power as internecine squabbles have riven our two main political parties; the thrust has ceased to be the national interest and become instead the cult of the individual.

If there is a common theme that links the *Henry VI*s with today, it is the fractious rivalry and petty squabbling that has characterised the Conservative and Labour Parties as it did the Houses of York and Lancaster. The lack of belief in collective achievement paved the way for both Richard III and Margaret Thatcher. John of Gaunt's other Eden of long ago was indeed leased out 'as to a tenement farm', in hock to ruthless ambition that served individual interest and favoured the strong. The days of Henry V and the British Empire, of former national glories, became, in both instances, distant, sun-kissed memories lingering on only in heightened myth and Little England xenophobia. The common good sacrificed on the altar of self.

It might not have happened if the throne had not been in the care of a Protector – Humphrey, Duke of Gloucester, the situation complicated by the attempt of the various factions to gain control of the young king. In reality, Henry was only a child when attaining the throne; in the play he's already coming up to adulthood, giving more dramatic scope to the weakness of his reign. As Gloucester and Winchester, Somerset and Warwick struggle for ascendancy, Henry himself anticipates the consequences of such self obsession:

> O, what a scandal is it to our crown
> That two such noble peers as ye should jar!
> Believe me, lords, my tender years can tell
> Civil dissension is a viperous worm

That gnaws the bowels of the commonwealth.
(*Part 1*, Act III.1)

But it is left to Exeter to set the in-fighting in context:

But howsoe'er, no simple man that sees
This jarring discord of nobility . . .
But that it doth presage some ill event.
'Tis much when sceptres are in children's hands;
But more when envy breeds unkind division.
There comes the ruin, there begins confusion.
(Act IV.1)

Although written after the *Henry VIs*, the death of Henry V – 'this star of England' – and the internecine strife that followed, is foreshadowed in the Chorus's final speech:

Small time, but in that small most greatly lived
This star of England. Fortune made his sword,
By which the world's best garden he achieved,
And of it left his son imperial lord.
Henry the Sixth, in infant bands crown'd King
Of France and England, did this king succeed,
Whose state so many had the managing
That they lost France and made his England bleed . . .
(*Henry V*, Epilogue)

Henry is hardly cold in his coffin when the family squabbles start:

WINCHESTER: He was a king blessed of the King of Kings.
Upon the French the dreadful Judgement Day
So dreadful will not be as was his sight.
The battle of the Lord of Hosts he fought;
The Church's prayers made him so prosperous.

GLOUCESTER: The Church? Where is it? Had not churchmen prayed,

His thread of life had not so soon decayed.
(*Part 1*, Act I.1)

And by *Part 2* France has gone with barely a flick of the eyebrow to acknowledge its passing:

KING: Welcome, Lord Somerset. What news from France?

SOMERSET: That all your interest in those territories
Is utterly bereft you; all is lost

KING: Cold news, Lord Somerset; but God's will be done!

YORK: *(aside)* Cold news for me; for I had hope of France
As firmly as I had hope for fertile England.
(*Part 2*, Act III.1)

Thus the dramatic action of *Part 1* polarises into two conflicting interests - internecine squabbles at home and the war with France abroad. As the struggle rages around the weak king, the stage is set for the rise of Shakespeare's most engaging villain, the Duke of York's youngest son, Richard of Gloucester. Thus the plays encompass in their entire sweep the collapse of idealism and the onset of materialism as lost eras of chivalry and honour are mourned over, even as those mourning take pragmatic action to ensure that they never return. Romanticism morphs into brutal realism: Richard II to Bolingbroke; Hotspur to Hal and Prince John; Talbot and son into Margaret and Suffolk; all of them into Richard III. Falstaff's rejection of honour in *Henry IV, Part 1* stands at the door of this charnel house holding up a sign for all that enter to abandon God and principle.

Guarding the door is a soldier as popular and renowned in his time as Wellington, Nelson, Montgomery . . . Talbot stands four-square as the ideal heroic warrior, fighting by the book, upholding ancient chivalric codes of birth and fame – an ideal which the French violate:

. . . Base muleteers of France!
Like peasant footboys do they keep the walls

And dare not take up arms like gentlemen.
(*Part 1*, Act III.2)

Gentlemen fight with swords, not with guns, and with one arm behind the back.

Rather than fight and run away to live and fight another day, his son, John Talbot, inherits his father's romantic set of rules of engagement with the inevitable consequences. Beaten back by the French, outnumbered, Talbot pleads with son John to save himself.

TALBOT: If we both stay, we both are sure to die.

JOHN: Then let me stay, and, father, do you fly.
Upon my death the French can little boast;
In yours they will; in you all hopes are lost.
Flight cannot stain the honour you have won;

TALBOT: And leave my followers here to fight alone?
My age was never tainted with such shame.

JOHN: And shall my youth be guilty of such blame?
No more can I be severed from you side
Than can yourself yourself in twain divide.
Stay, go, do what you will – the like do I;
For live, I will not if my father die.
(Act IV.6)

As at the Somme, the American War of Independence, or the Valley of Death, so England is defeated by the intransigent stubbornness of a leader who fought by the book and eschewed tactics. In Act IV.4, Somerset's is a lone voice raised against the wholesale adulation heaped on Talbot's life and death:

SOMERSET: This expedition was by York and Talbot
Too rashly plotted . . .
. . . The over-daring Talbot
Hath sullied all his gloss of former honour

By this unheedful, desperate, wild adventure.
(Act IV.4)

The French, a bunch of cads, have no such compunction about playing the game. Rouen is captured by soldiers disguised as peasants and at Orléans the English leaders are picked off by snipers. Rather than reading this as anti-French propaganda, it is better to look at it in the context of all's fair in war. If you want to win, there are no rules. The French won. No point looking down your nose. This is particularly true of the contrast between the two main protagonists – a bastard peasant girl versus an aristocratic nobleman; evasion and trickery versus old-fashioned heroics. And in contrast with John Talbot, Joan is ready to reject both her father and her family to save her neck. Even her name – *la Pucelle* – has in it implicit irony, the word meaning both virgin and whore. After her capture and burning at the stake, the marriage of Henry to Margaret of Anjou is greeted as an act of gross betrayal of the English cause and the concluding of an 'effeminate peace' something that degrades and dishonours the memory of the fallen. Richard is not alone when he displays disgust at the idea of Henry's French nuptials.

RICHARD: . . . After the slaughter of so many peers,
So many captains, gentlemen and soldiers
That in this quarrel have been overthrown
And sold their bodies for their country's benefit . . .
(Act V.4)

This is Joan of Arc's posthumous revenge. Talbot, Salisbury and Bedford may represent an aristocratic Old Boys' club, but it is Joan and the French who embody the new political reality, setting Shakespeare's agenda for the rest of the canon. We await the growth of Richard III, passing through some pretty awesome Machiaveli on the way.

* * *

The *Henry VI*s are notable for the emergence for the first time on stage of female power. Indeed, the plays have often been pressed into service to advance the cause of feminism. All three female characters in *Part 1* attempt to rule their menfolk – often by sorcery. This has been seen as proof that Shakespeare was a misogynist – a women-hater. This ignores the social context of a world where real power was invested solely in the hands of men. It is hardly surprising that women resorted to desperate measures in order to achieve some crumb of equality.

Two female figures dominate the action. If Joan of Arc – Joan la Pucelle – looms over *Henry VI, Part 1*, then Margaret of Anjou – Queen Margaret – emerges as a potent political force in *Henry VI, Parts 2* and *3*.

Trading on the audience's belief in the occult and the supernatural, Shakespeare allows the character of Joan to be the victim of a massive dollop of Elizabethan propaganda, investing her with the qualities of a witch – 'A disciple and limb of the Fiend . . . that used false enchantment and sorcery'. But it was not witchcraft that defeated the Dauphin but brilliant sword play, so it is hardly surprising that having faced down the entire English army the humiliated leaders believe that the only way they could have lost the battle was through sorcery. (Rather like Sir Clive Woodward explaining away the rugby annihilation in 2005 of the British Lions by the All Blacks as being due to the spear tackle on the captain, O'Driscoll in the first minute of the first test.) 'The holy maid' sees herself as something else – the saviour of France – and if no male is going to step up to the plate then a woman will. And Shakespeare gives her the power of oratory so to do. No sorcery there, only eloquent language, such as that used by Henry V to exhort his troops into one final push into the breach; language that convinces Burgundy not to fight on the side of the English but to return to the fold. 'Look on thy country, look on fertile France,' she begs.

> **LA PUCELLE: . . . And see the cities and the towns defac'd**
> **By wasting ruin of the cruel foe;**
> **As looks the mother on her lowly babe**
> **When death doth close his tender dying eyes,**
> **See, see the pining malady of France;**
> **Behold the wounds, the most unnatural wounds,**
> **Which thou thyself has give her woeful breast.**
> **(*Part 1*, Act III.5)**

Burgundy is persuaded – 'Either she hath bewitch'd me with her words or nature makes me suddenly relent'. 'Done like a Frenchman,' Joan says and then adds an aside guaranteed to get a laugh from the groundlings but dangerous to attribute to Shakespeare rather than an actor looking for a cheap rise – 'Turn and turn again'.

Described at first as a shepherdess and a prophet, Joan is caricatured and parodied throughout the play as the converse of the English hero, Talbot (it is said that strong men wept at his death in Act IV). The two characters stand in apposition throughout the play, albeit stylistically from a totally different perspective. Where Talbot is treated with dignity and respect, Joan is pilloried and degraded. Having declared, 'I must not yield to any rites of love/For my professions sacred from above' (Act I.2), she seduces the Dauphin (Act II.1). Where Talbot's death is heroic, Joan twists and lies in a desperate attempt to save her life. 'O, burn her, burn her: hanging is too good' (Act V.4), says her father. Not exactly a leaf out of the Talbots' familial bonding book. She claims virginity, then pregnancy identifying some half dozen fathers; when all else fails, she curses. For her, as for Falstaff, honour is a mere scutcheon. What use is it if you're dead? Leave that to the Talbots. The brazenness of her fabrications to save her neck (and France) is refreshingly shameless. Better to be expedient. In war, idealism has no place. With or without the aid of the supernatural, there is still a battle to be fought where men will die for real. No point sitting on your fanny waiting for a miracle to happen. She is acutely aware of her mortality. As she says to the Dauphin:

> **LA PUCELLE: At all times will you have my power alike?**
> **Sleeping or waking, must I still prevail,**
> **Or will you blame and lay the fault on me?**
> **Improvident soldiers! Had your watch been good**
> **This sudden mischief never could have fall'n.**
> **(Act II.1)**

No saint, but no witch either. More a tough, street-fighting girl for whom the realities of war demand a certain kind of behaviour. And if myth and magic help the cause so much the better. Instead, in a messy ending, the English defeat Joan by ganging up on her. But the triumph is shortlived. This was to be their last success in France.

Margaret of Anjou is another kettle of *poisson*. Sorcery and witchcraft of another kind. Acting the pimp, Suffolk wins her for Henry's hand with a titillating seductive litany of her qualities and then falls for her himself. Thus he becomes a power behind the weak throne, secure in the sexual favours of the queen, safe in the knowledge that the naïve, ineffectual Henry would suspect nothing. Margaret is a prototype Macbeth, a female counterpart of Richard of Gloucester, by whom she is outwitted but whom she outlives. York, no angel himself, rails against her:

> She wolf of France . . .
> O tiger's heart wrapped in a woman's hide!
> How couldst thou drain the life-blood of the child,
> To bid the father wipe his eyes withal,
> And yet be seen to bear a woman's face?
> Women are soft, mild, pitiful, and flexible;
> Thou stern, obdurate, flinty, rough, remorseless.
> Biddest thou me rage? Why, now thou hast thy wish;
> Wouldst have me weep? Why, now thou hast thy will;
> For raging wind blows up incessant showers,
> And when the rage allays, the rain begins.
> (*Part 3*, Act I.4)

As Margaret has just wiped his face with a napkin steeped in the blood of Rutland, his murdered son, York's rage is somewhat understandable; yet he himself has been guilty of callous acts in the course of his quest for the throne. His words are wild and whirling, the emotion running the gamut, the histrionic actor demonstrating the highs and lows of rhetorical passion. Margaret teaches York a lesson in brutal callousness. Waiting until his tirade is over and his passion spent in incoherent weeping, she says, 'And here's to right our gentle hearted king' and stabs him. And:

> Off with his head, and set it on York gates;
> So York may overlook the town of York.

* * *

If civil war is a domestic struggle to ascertain what kind of government the people desire for themselves, then anyone can play. Midway between the death of Gloucester and the start of the Wars of the Roses, the boys are joined by an unlikely figure from the common folk – Jack Cade. The original Cade Rebellion, born of genuine grievances, had the support of the landowners and gentry. In *Henry VI, Part 2* we are confronted by a man gathering to his standard the illiterate and uneducated under the pretence that he is the rightful heir to the throne. The measures that he would institute would warm the cockles of the New Brutalists. The lawyers would all be killed, there would be no more reading and writing, and henceforth the laws would all come out of his mouth. The Tories would have loved him. Home Secretary in no time. The only thing a bit *de trop* maybe, would be having the 'pissing conduit' run with red claret.

This dynamic trouble-maker from Kent has been enlisted by York to aid his cause by gathering around him a large contingent of peasants who are encouraged to revolt on the promise of plenty.

CADE: Be brave, then, for your captain is brave, and vows reformation. There shall be in England seven halfpenny loaves sold for a penny; the three-hooped pot shall have ten hoops; and I will make it felony to drink small beer. All the realm shall be in common, and in Cheapside shall my palfrey go to grass. And when I am king, as king I will be –

ALL: God save your majesty!

CADE: I thank you, good people. There shall be no money; all shall eat and drink on my score; and I will apparel them all in one livery, that they may agree like brothers and worship me their lord.
(*Henry VI, Part 2*, Act IV.2)

Shakespeare's portrait of the common people is hardly a flattering one. And his version of this Kentish rebellion is somewhat unbelievable. (There has always been a pocket of insurrection in this plummy heartland of English garden conservatism. In 1985 the Kent miners, all six thousand of them, were the last to capitulate). The people are dimwitted, fickle, destructive, galvanised into action at the thought of rich pickings but are cowed and give up easily when threatened.

The whole episode has the atmosphere of a demented carnival about it. York's description of Cade stuck full of weapons conjures up the image of a grotesque Morris dancer:

> **. . . I have seen**
> **Him caper upright like a wild Morisco,**
> **Shaking the bloody darts as he his bells.**
> (*Part 2*, Act III.1)

This frenzied carnival spirit runs right through the rebellion, giving Cade a wild anarchic power. There is something alluring in the mumbo-jumbo of his mixed-up philosophy, an appeal to popular grievances that would have found many takers in his audience – lower taxes, lower prices (inflation was a big Elizabethan issue), but most of all, power in the hands of the people. This pot pourri of communism, fascism, theocracy and free booze had an instant attraction about it. And the promise of direct action to cure all their ills rallied many of the poor to the cause. Who wouldn't thrill at the idea of setting 'London Bridge afire, and if you can the Tower too'? The grassroots rebellion, timed and linked as it is to a shady Yorkist cause, offers a picture of power at its most fluid and its most dangerous. Amidst all the absurdity of the affair is a serious threat to government and civil order. If not contained, then anarchy will rule and York and his followers would have been hard pushed to bring the rebels back into line once they'd tasted popular power. When the mob go on the rampage in *Julius Caesar*, the flames, fanned by Antony's oratory, send the fire out of control. The mob seek out the leaders responsible for Caesar's assassination. They come across Cinna, not the conspirator, but the poet. They kill him anyway, for his rotten poetry.

This same danger of indiscriminate retribution runs through the Cade revolt. The attack on Lord Say, sent to try and negotiate, is most chilling:

> **CADE: . . . Thou has most traitorously corrupted the youth of**
> **the realm in erecting a grammar school; and whereas, before,**
> **our forefathers had no other books but the score and the tally,**

thou hast caused printing to be used; and, contrary to the King, his crown, and dignity, thou hast built a paper-mill. It will be proved to thy face that thou hast men about thee that usually talk of a noun and a verb, and such abominable words as no Christian ear can endure to hear. Thou hast appointed justices of peace, to call poor men before them about matters they were not able to answer. Moreover, thou hast put them in prison; and because they could not read, thou hast hanged them; when, indeed, only for that cause they have been most worthy to live . . .
(*Part 2*, Act IV.7)

There are genuine grievances here. We are reminded of how privilege and elitism look from outside the circle by those who are not part of that inner coterie. Culture and civilisation seem to be under attack here, but in a society where a man can be hanged merely for not being able to read, it is small wonder that those who are illiterate through no fault of their own revolt. History has not confined this apparent philistinism to the mass. Zahir Hadid's stunning design for the Cardiff Opera House was sunk by a virulent campaign against opera as an elitist pursuit by the current First Secretary of Wales and the then Lord Mayor. Cardiff got a rugby stadium instead.

We are reminded that Shakespeare may not often give voice to the commoner, but when he does, it is usually to articulate social injustice. The ludicrous interlude of the blind and crippled Simpcox, who is tricked by Gloucester into seeing and jumping, has a serious intent. As they are hustled off, Simpcox's wife cries out, 'Alas! sir, we did it for pure need' (Act II.1).

Cade at such moments becomes one of Shakespeare's most articulate social critics, but the problem with such a mixed-up philosophy – a cross between democratic utopianism and fascist dictatorship – is that it has no rules other than its own. The Clerk of Chatham is dragged off to be hanged with his pen and ink horn about his neck, merely for being able to read and keep accounts; Lord Say's head is severed and put on a pole so that he and his son-in-law may kiss. It is significant that Cade's most prominent sidekick and voluble supporter is Dick the Butcher, author of the most memorable line of the play: 'The first thing we do, let's kill all the lawyers'. Guaranteed to get a standing ovation.

As his sense of power grows, so Cade's targets progress from attacking the rich to attacking anyone who has something he desires:

> **The proudest peer in the realm shall not wear a head on his shoulders, unless he pay me tribute; there shall not a maid be married, but she shall pay to me her maidenhead, ere they have it.**

It is ironic that the very era that Cade evokes as England's golden age, the reign of Henry V, is the very thing that undoes him. He says to the Staffords, also attempting to negotiate – I use the term loosely – 'Rebellious hinds, the filth and scum of Kent . . . ':

> **CADE: . . . Go to, sirrah, tell the King from me that for his father's sake, Henry the Fifth, in whose time boys went to span-counter for French crowns, I am content he shall reign; but I'll be Protector over him.**

> **DICK: And furthermore we'll have the Lord Say's head for selling the dukedom of Maine.**

> **CADE: . . . And more than that, he can speak French . . .**
> **(*Part 2*, Act IV.2)**

At a third attempt, Clifford convinces the rabble to return to their homes by appealing to that same patriotic, xenophobic fear of foreigners. Contemptuously dismissing Cade, Clifford says,

> **Will he conduct you through the heart of France,**
> **And make the meanest of you earls and dukes?**
> **(Act IV.8)**

And home they go. Cade is left to ponder on the shifting sands of popular support. 'Was ever feather so lightly blown to and fro as this multitude? The name of Henry the Fifth hales them to an hundred mischiefs, and leaves me desolate'. The last we see of him he is eating grass. But with his disappearance, a light goes out of the play and his dying boast – 'Tell Kent from me, she hath lost her best man' – strikes a chord with audiences, left once again with the aristocratic mayhem of yet more battles for the hollow crown.

* * *

Wakefield, Towton, Barnet and Tewkesbury. These are the battles at the heart of the action of the three plays. In real life, over 50,000 men died at Towton, more than had ever died on British soil before or since. In one simple, devastating scene, Shakespeare characterises the senseless slaughter, the inconsequential futility of these civil broils. Henry, seeking solitude and solace away from the battlefield, sits on a molehill and muses on the impotence of kingship. He longs for a simple existence away from the responsibility of the cares of state:

> **O God! methinks it were a happy life**
> **To be no better than a homely swain;**
> **To sit upon a hill, as I do now,**
> **To carve out dials quaintly, point by point,**
> **Thereby to see the minutes how they run:**
> **How many makes the hour full complete,**
> **How many hours brings about the day,**
> **How many days will finish up the year,**
> **How many years a mortal man may live.**
> **When this is known, then to divide the times:**
> **So many hours must I tend my flock,**
> **So many hours must I make my rest,**
> **So many hours must I contemplate,**
> **So many hours must I sport myself,**
> **So many days my ewes have been with young,**
> **So many weeks ere the poor fools will ean,**
> **So many years ere I shall shear the fleece.**
> **So minutes, hours, days, months, and years,**
> **Passed over to the end they were created,**
> **Would bring white hairs unto a quiet grave.**
> **Ah, what a life were this! How sweet! How lovely!**
> **(*Part 3*, Act II.5)**

A man enters lugging a body which he hopes to rob, but removing the helmet he makes a grim discovery. 'Who's this?' he cries:

> **. . . O God! It is my father's face,**
> **Whom in this conflict I, unwares, have killed.**
> **O, heavy times, begetting such events!**

As if this irony were not enough, from the other side of the stage another man enters, this time a father carrying the body of his son.

> **O pity, God, this miserable age!**
> **What stratagems, how fell, how butcherly,**
> **Erroneous, mutinous, and unnatural,**
> **This deadly quarrel daily doth beget!**

The folly and impossibility of Henry's fantasy is exposed as he witnesses the dead sons and fathers. He cries out:

> **KING HENRY: Woe above woe! Grief more than common grief!**
> **O that my death would stay these ruthful deeds!**
> **O, pity, pity, gentle heaven, pity!**
> **The red rose and the white are on his face,**
> **The fatal colours of our striving houses . . .**

York, Lancaster, white rose, red – What did it mean? Where was God in all this? Divine right . . . The scene has a savage beauty. The breakdown of moral order. While Henry sits on a molehill and longs for the life of a simple shepherd, the reality of the chaos he has helped create surrounds him. It is a familiar royal lament. Richard II and Henry V both, at moments of extreme personal crisis, cry out for the balm of a simple existence. But the reality is other. For Richard II it is assassination, for Henry it is Agincourt.

* * *

At the heart of *Part 1* and the next three plays lies the scene in the Temple garden, one of the few scenes for which there does not appear to be any factual basis. The garden metaphor prevalent in Richard II is here taken up once again as flowers become the symbol of governance. In diverting the plot away from mangled history, Shakespeare finds a flight of poetic imagination conspicuously lacking in most of *Part 1*. The action is driven on by Richard Plantagenet, Richard of Gloucester, later Richard III. As early as Act II.4, we see the emergence of the confrontational style that is to bewitch and bother the course of England in the next period of time:

> **RICHARD: Great lords and gentlemen, what means this**
> **silence?**
> **Dare no man answer in a case of truth?**
>
> **SUFFOLK: Within the Temple Hall we were too loud;**
> **The garden here is more convenient.**
>
> **RICHARD: Then say at once if I maintained the truth;**
> **Or else was wrangling in Somerset in th'error?**
>
> **SUFFOLK: Faith, I have been a truant in the law**
> **And never yet could frame my will to it;**
> **And therefore frame the law unto my will.**
>
> **SOMERSET: Judge you, my lord of Warwick, then between us.**

Warwick produces the ultimate in fence-sitting –

> **WARWICK: Between two hawks, which flies the higher pitch;**
> **Between two dogs, which hath the deeper mouth;**
> **Between two blades, which bears the better temper;**
> **Between two horses, which doth bear him best;**
> **Between two girls, which hath the merriest eye,**
> **I have perhaps some shallow spirit of judgement;**
> **But in these nice sharp quillets of the law,**
> **Good faith, I am no wiser than a daw . . .**

– But Richard is having none of it. He's feeling punchy.

RICHARD: Since you are tongue-tied and so loath to speak,
In dumb significants proclaim your thoughts.
Let him that is a true-born gentleman
And stands upon the honour of his birth,
If he suppose that I have pleaded truth,
From off this briar pluck a white rose with me.

SOMERSET: Let him that is no coward nor no flatterer,
But dare maintain the party of the truth,
Pluck a red rose from off this thorn with me.

Somerset calls him a liar. Warwick immediately jumps off the fence:

WARWICK: I love no colours; and, without all colour
Of base insinuating flattery,
I pluck this white rose with Plantagenet.

SUFFOLK: I pluck this red rose with young Somerset,
And say withal I think he held the right.
(Act II.4)

Two all.

And so they're off and running. The lawyer comes down on Richard's side, giving him the legal nod. It's a moot point as to whether it would have made any difference had the lawyer opted for Somerset – the die is cast; red and white roses merely an excuse for prosecuting the argument. Thus far, Richard is seen only as a younger son upholding the honour of his family. The monster is yet to come.

The way is paved by Suffolk. At the conclusion of *Part 1* he discloses his motives, Richard-like.

SUFFOLK: Thus Suffolk hath prevailed; and thus he goes,
As did the youthful Paris once to Greece,
With hope to find the event in love
But prosper better than the Trojan did.
Margaret shall now be Queen, and rule the King;

But I will rule both her, the King, and realm.
(Part 1, Act V.5)

In *Part 2* Suffolk emerges as a man devoid of all sense of political responsibility, a fitting companion for Margaret, the two of them hell-bent on ruthlessly manipulating the course of England's destiny from behind the weak throne, partners in amorous amorality. Henry's sexual inadequacy propels Margaret into Suffolk's bed, the place she believes will lead to the power she craves. It was a huge disappointment to find that, far from ruling England, she is surrounded by feuding noblemen, each with an ambitious agenda to fulfil. They are obstacles in her path, none more so than the king's Protector, Gloucester, and his wife:

QUEEN: . . . As that proud dame, the Lord Protector's wife.
She sweeps it through the court with troops of ladies,
More like an empress than Duke Humphrey's wife.
Strangers in court do take her for the queen.
She bears a duke's revenues on her back,
And in her heart she scorns our poverty.
Shall I not live to be avenged on her?
(Part 2, Act I.3)

The sharks, scenting blood, have gathered:

GLOUCESTER: . . . A heart unspotted is not easily daunted.
The purest spring is not so free from mud
As I am clear from treason to my sovereign.
(Act III.1)

Gloucester was a naïve, an innocent; the guiltless need fear no danger. He just didn't get it. But Margaret backed the wrong horse. Suffolk's duplicity and his bid for ultimate power was always going to end in disaster, and it was only a matter of time before the efforts of the fighting factions, once they had got rid of the Gloucesters, turned their attention his way. Do we feel any sympathy for Margaret as she cradles the severed head of Suffolk?

QUEEN: Here may his head lie on my throbbing breast;
But where's the body that I should embrace?
(Act IV.4)

I don't think so.

Parts 2 and *3* show once again the dangers of hiding behind dodgy legal advice as an excuse for going to war, and the consequences of such duplicity. Attempting to apply a moral wash to actions that are plainly illegal leads only to the breakdown of moral order. The repercussions of the war in Iraq have led to the excesses of Guantanamo Bay, Abu Graib and the slaughter of thousands of innocent Iraqi civilians. When big men fight it is the little who get caught in the crossfire. The disintegration of society into chaos is a consequence of politicians eager to hide duplicitous actions behind a veil of self-justification. Thus in *Part 2*, Gloucester's enemies are eager to convince themselves and the world of the righteousness of their behaviour. By *Part 3*, moral order has broken down and trust is nowhere to be found. Characters continually lie for their own ends and go back on their word; oaths are broken right, left and centre, and loyalty lasts only as long as a player is on the way up. A new breed of power broker is on the scene. Richard of Gloucester defines existential *real politik* thus –

But for a kingdom any oath may be broken;
I will break a thousand oaths to reign one year.

This ethical vacuum was made for Richard, much as political and civil chaos, throughout history, have bred other such tyrants. 'Order', it seems, can only be restored by strong measures, the people subdued and brought into line by brute force and the elimination of dissent. And in Richard's case, his mental distortion is mirrored by his physical; indeed, he patently revels in his indigested and deformed shape.

It comes as a surprise to discover that Richard was not always the captivating monster who has thrilled and delighted audiences for 400 years. Your starter for ten – who said the following?

> See how the morning opes her golden gates,
> And takes her farewell of the glorious sun!
> How well resembles it the prime of youth,
> Trimmed like a younker prancing to his love!

Wrong. It was the young Richard (*Part 3*, Act II.1). In the beginning, there is no hint of the tyrant to come and it is not until Act III.2, that we get the first suggestion that it is a psychological reaction to his deformity that drives his ruthless quest for the crown:

> RICHARD: . . . Then, since this earth affords no joy to me
> But to command, to check, to o'erbear such
> As are of better person than myself,
> I'll make my heaven to dream upon the crown . . .
> (*Part 3*, Act III.2)

Just as Johnny Depp distorts Willy Wonka's callousness in the film of *Charlie and the Chocolate Factory* by attributing his heartlessness to a loveless childhood, so Shakespeare distorts Richard's motives by making his handicap an amoral virtue:

> Why, love forswore me in my mother's womb;
> And, for I should not deal in her soft laws,
> She did corrupt frail nature with some bribe
> To shrink mine arm up like a withered shrub;
> To make an envious mountain on my back,
> Where sits deformity to mock my body . . .

Mae Rose Cottage says in *Under Milk Wood*[3], 'I'll sin till I blow up'. Richard, too, is concerned with sin on an inhuman scale of myth-making proportions:

> I'll drown more sailors than the mermaid shall;
> I'll slay more gazers than the basilisk;
> I'll play the orator as well as Nestor,
> Deceive more slily than Ulysses could,
> And, like a Sinon, take another Troy.

> I can add colours to chameleon,
> Change shapes with Protheus for advantages,
> And set the murderous Machiavel to school.
> (*Part 3*, Act III.2)

However, it is Henry VI who gives the myth substance, accurately fingering the dark future that England is about to face:

> And thus I prophesy, that many a thousand,
> Which now mistrust no parcel of my fear,
> And many an old man's sigh, and many a widow's,
> And many an orphan's water-standing eye –
> Men for their sons', wives for their husbands',
> And orphans for their parents' timeless death –
> Shall rue the hour that ever thou wast born.
> The owl shrieked at thy birth, aboding luckless time;
> Dogs howled, and hideous tempest shook down trees . . .
> (Act V.6)

Henry's prophesy gives Richard a new apocalyptic dimension. Richard has only one aim – to get the crown – and to do that he will kill as many people as he needs to kill. The crown matters and mattered little to Henry, and in death as in life his piety as a Christian shines through. As far as he is concerned, Richard has come 'to bite the world'. And at that moment, Richard kills him.

> RICHARD: I'll hear not more; die, prophet; in thy speech!
> *He Stabs him.*
> For this, amongst the rest, was I ordained.
>
> KING HENRY: Aye, and for much more slaughter after this.
> O, God, forgive my sins, and pardon thee!
>
> *He dies.*

Metaphorically sitting on the body of the dead king, Richard muses on the truth of his predictions:

The midwife wondered; and the women cried
'O, Jesus bless us, he is born with teeth!'
And so I was, which plainly signified
That I should snarl and bite and play the dog.
Then, since the heavens have shap'd my body so,
Let hell make crooked my mind to answer it.
I have no brother, I am like no brother;
And this word 'love', which greybeards call divine,
Be resident in men like one another
And not in me; I am myself alone.

I am myself alone. I kill therefore I am. Echoes of Franz Moor in Schiller's *Die Raüber* — God forgive me, I am no ordinary murderer. Richard isolates himself from the conflicts around him. He even distances himself from his father, whose sole ambition it was to restore the House of York to the throne. But Richard is interested in power simply for its own sake, and the action is now no longer about the struggle of the two great Houses of York and Lancaster; it is about the complete breakdown of moral order, where the man of no belief tears up the rule book and rips apart the bonds of blood. The *frisson* of excitement will be rewarded for us in the next play.

Notes

1. *Green's Groatsworth of Wit, Bought with a Million of Repentance*, Pamphlet 1592.
2. *Shakespeare's Political Drama*, Alexander Legatt, Routledge, London 1988.
3. By Dylan Thomas.

Richard III

God say Amen

For a play that contains one of the world's great charismatic, quintessential villains, *Richard III* is pretty impenetrable. If you don't know what's gone on in the previous seven plays, haven't read it, had it explained to you, are seeing it for the first time, then a good third is unintelligible.

> RICHARD: Now is the winter of our discontent
> Made glorious summer by this sun of York,
> And all the clouds that loured upon our house
> In the deep bosom of the ocean buried.
> Now are our brows bound with victorious wreaths,
> Our bruisèd arms hung up for monuments,
> Our stern alarums changed to merry meetings,
> Our dreadful marches to delightful measures.
> Grim-visaged war hath smoothed his wrinkled front,
> And now, instead of mounting barbèd steeds
> To fright the souls of fearful adversaries,
> He capers nimbly in a lady's chamber
> To the lascivious pleasing of a lute.
> (Act I.1)

What on earth does all that mean? No use looking in your Arden notes to see that the winter of discontent has nothing to do with Callaghan's misery, or that the sun of York is a dynastical pun. Sure, you can get the general gist of it, but without knowledge (and concentration in the very first minute of the play) the nuance and subtlety are lost. And who on earth is that batty old bag Margaret? What's she on?

> Hear me, you wrangling pirates, that fall out
> In sharing that which you have pilled from me!

Which of you trembles not that looks on me?
If not, that I am Queen you bow like subjects,
Yet that, by you deposed, you quake like rebels?
. . . I do find more pain in banishment
Than death can yield me here by my abode.
A husband and a son thou ow'st to me –
And thou a kingdom – all of you allegiance.
This sorrow that I have, by right is yours,
And all the pleasure you usurp are mine.
Did York's dread curse prevail so much with heaven
. . . That Henry's death, my lovely Edward's death,
Their kingdom's loss, my woeful banishment,
Should all but answer for that peevish brat?
Can curses pierce the clouds and enter heaven?
Why then, give way, dull clouds, to my quick curses!
(Act I.3)

Were Elizabethan audiences more knowledgeable about their own history than we are today? Richard III was defeated at Bosworth some seventy odd years before Shakespeare was born. Going back to tell the story of Richard II is the equivalent for us of going back to about 1750. In a world where today 25% of young people can't even name the current Prime Minister, it's a pretty safe bet that Wellington's legacy is simply a load of old boots. Is a folk memory and an oral tradition stronger than an electronic one? I believe an audience's knowledge of anything other than their recent history has always been pretty patchy and four hundred years ago, with no mass media to inform and literacy confined to a very few, the chances of anything other than a wholly inaccurate version of the past were pretty slim. What must have made the difference in the theatre, then, was a fascination with the Elizabethan equivalent of a soap opera. For *Eastenders* and the Windsors, read *Shakespeare's Serial History Plays* – The Plantaganets Versus the Tudors. At a time when the population of London was not much more that 150,000, compared with today an extraordinarily high percentage could be found at any one time inside a theatre, hungry for the next episode in the ongoing dynastical saga of England's war crimes. When James Burbage, Theatre Manager, elder brother of Richard Burbage, the leading actor in Shakespeare's company, invented the box office, bringing bystanders off the streets and corralling them in the wooden Os of the newly-invented theatres, he created an unprecedented demand. And what you couldn't see for free you were determined to pay for, in case you missed anything. Similar to Sky, really, buying up world rights for sporting events. If you want to see it, pay for it. The Elizabethans did, in their thousands. Mind you. It must have been pretty confusing getting the histories out of order – the *Henry VI*s and *Richard III* preceding the *Henry IV*s and *Henry V*, and then *Richard II* tagged onto the end of *Richard III* – 5, 6, 7, 8, 1, 2, 3, 4. It certainly accounts, when played in chronological order, for the disjointed style of the language and the odd story-telling technique. Shakespeare's mastery of the material reaches a psychological depth by the time he reaches 'the skipping king' that was almost non-existent in the *Henry VI*s. But at least the figure of Richard Crookback followed on sequentially, allowing us to enjoy the full flavour of his ascent to the throne.

Despite coming out of order, *Richard III* is the natural culmination of two tetralogies, spanning the 100 years from Richard II, of bloody slaughter in the name of divine right. Brother kills brother, mother betrays son, cousin fights cousin, father slaughters son, all in the name of 'the golden round', 'the hollow crown', 'a little brief authority', proving – if it ever needed proving – that blood is not thicker than water when it comes to the exercise and possession of raw, naked power:

> **DUCHESS OF YORK: Accursèd and unquiet wrangling days,**
> **How many of you have mine eyes beheld!**
> **My husband lost his life to get the crown,**
> **And often up and down my sons were tossed**
> **For me to joy and weep their gain and loss;**
> **And being seated, and domestic broils**
> **Clean overblown, themselves the conquerors**
> **Make war upon themselves, brother to brother,**
> **Blood to blood, self against self. O preposterous**
> **And frantic outrage, end thy damnèd spleen,**
> **Or let me die, to look on earth no more!**
> **(Act II.4)**

Is this slaughter divine? Henry V attributes the carnage at Agincourt of 10,000 French dead to twenty-nine English to an act of God. Richmond, at the end of *Richard III*, prays to the Almighty to give him the strength in his right arm to kill as many of his enemies as possible. Once again, it takes a butcher to beat a butcher – a Churchill to overcome a Hitler, a Bush to beat a Hussein. (Don't mention Bin Laden). Ruthless pragmatism, superior numbers, inferior tactics or more sophisticated fire power? If God is around, so much the better, but don't bank on it. Better get out the Bullworker, practise your place kicks. Won't do to have God standing by helplessly as you miss a penalty. Richard understands this. He is the quintessential man of action. The one who says, 'This is what I'm going to do', and does it.

> He cannot live, I hope, and must not die
> Till George be packed with post-horse up to heaven.
> I'll in, to urge his hatred more to Clarence
> With lies well steeled with weighty arguments;
> And, if I fail not in my deep intent,
> Clarence hath not another day to live;
> Which done, God take King Edward to His mercy
> And leave the world for me to bustle in!
> For then I'll marry Warwick's youngest daughter.
> What though I killed her husband and her father?
> The readiest way to make the wench amends
> Is to become her husband and her father,
> The which I will – not all so much for love
> As for another secret close intent
> By marrying her which I must reach unto.
> But yet I run before my horse to market:
> Clarence still breathes; Edward still lives and reigns;
> When they are gone, then must I count my gains.
> (Act I.1)

At a time when the authority of the Church held the world in awe of its power, where fear of retribution in this life and after held sway, and superstition bred terror in ready minds, the man of no belief in anything other than existential action is a killer. And if he has a smile on his face at the same time, we love him. Until we, too, succumb to his savagery. Sharing knowledge and insight with Richard, even sympathising with him against our better judgement, we are not just detached spectators: Richard enlists us as his accomplices and, like the character of Vice in the old morality plays, presents himself as a friend to the audience. But, as the play develops, we discover that this friend is not to be trusted. Appalled, we realise that we have let him get away with murder – literally. ('One person can make a difference and every person must try' – JFK.) It is easier to stand by, do nothing, appease, rather than stick one's neck out and risk having it cut off.

Life has mirrored art in giving us a distorted historical view of Richard, our knowledge almost entirely governed by Shakespeare's play. Will the real *Richard III* please stand up? Is it the one with the hump and the withered arm, denounced by successive centuries as a child murderer and a ruthless butcher of wife and family? Or the 'good king', a propaganda victim of the over-arching ambitions and political skullduggery of the Tudors whose patronage, Shakespeare recognised, must butter his bread? The view of others – not mine.

Acres of paper have been covered in rationalising Richard's behaviour as a result of the debit in his psychological makeup caused by Shakespeare's depiction of his deformity. Not helped of course by Richard's own admission of his personal problem in coming to grips with his physical defects. We gather as much as early as *Henry VI, Part 3*, Act III.2, when he declares 'love foreswore me in my mother's womb' and resolving,

> . . . since this earth affords no joy to me
> But to command, to check, to o'erbear such
> As are of better person than myself,
> I'll make my heaven to dream upon the crown . . .

We are thus totally prepared for the amplification of this when immediately as part of his opening soliloquy in *Richard III* he turns and fixes us with his engaging grin and declares:

> But I, that am not shaped for sportive tricks
> Nor made to court an amorous looking-glass;

I, that am rudely stamped, and want love's majesty
To strut before a wanton ambling nymph;
I, that am curtailed of this fair proportion,
Cheated of feature by dissembling Nature,
Deformed, unfinished, sent before my time
Into this breathing world, scarce half made up,
And that so lamely and unfashionable
That dogs bark at me as I halt by them –
Why I, in this weak piping time of peace,
Have no delight to pass away the time,
Unless to spy my shadow in the sun
And descant on mine own deformity.
And therefore, since I cannot prove a lover
To entertain these fair well-spoken days,
I am determined to prove a villain
And hate the idle pleasures of these days.

Do we go Freud's route of the twisted adult bruised by childhood experience – bullying at school, jeering in the shower – and now hell-bent on revenge? Or is it hatred of his mother?

DUCHESS OF YORK: God bless thee, and put meekness in
thy breast,

Love, charity obedience and true duty!

RICHARD: Amen! *(Aside)* **And make me die a good old man!**
That is the butt-end of a mother's blessing;
I marvel that her grace did leave it out.
(Act II.2 ll 107-111)

Envy of his brother? ('Simple, plain Clarence, I do love thee so/That I will shortly send thy soul to heaven' Of the world? Whatever the cause, Richard's descant on his own deformity is a mocking self-cynicism that invites us to agree with him about how ugly he is, and therefore complicitly involves us in his deeds. Are the monstrous aspects of his appearance a reason or a pretext – merely an excuse in order to use them as a source of malevolent power?

As with other existential figures in Shakespeare, Richard is going along fine until doubt sets in. As long as the mind is moving forward, for men of action there is no problem. As soon as you start looking over your shoulder, that's the danger sign. The great poker player always plays the odds – is never tempted into a rash bet because of a hunch. That isn't to say that risks aren't taken, but along with that taken risk goes calculation. No leader ever lasted long merely by betting on certainties, but the better ones (notice I don't say 'good' – I'm not altogether sure what constitutes a 'good leader') know that nine times out of ten the risk that they take will pay off. Because the world believes that people are inherently 'good', it trusts the tiger with the wide grin, not recognising that the spread of the jaw is a prelude to devouring the onlooker. The Richard of action travels an almost obstacle-free path to the throne, the fox among the chickens. The Woodvilles and Greys make an awful lot of clucking, rushing around headless until the farmer arrives to sort it all out with his shotgun.

But the seed of Richard's downfall has already been planted in his own head. 'I could be bounded in a nutshell and count myself a king of infinite space were it not that I have bad dreams' (*Hamlet*, Act II.2). Richard has bad dreams (the play is notable for containing more references to dreams than any other of Shakespeare's plays. Apart from *The Tempest* – itself a dream). His infinite space disappears. He turns inward. Instead of setting about cementing his relationship with the country, outflanking his enemies by turning domestic politician, paranoia sets in. Like Macbeth before (or, rather, after) him, he is

> . . . in blood
> Stepped in so far, that, should I wade no more,
> Returning were as tedious as go o'er.
> (*Macbeth*, Act III.4)

and like Lady Macbeth, Buckingham can no longer follow where Richard leads. Both Lady Macbeth and Buckingham fail to understand the nature of the beast to which they are yoked. Neither sees beyond the point of achieving the throne. To stay there at the top demands the purge, the elimination, the Night of the Long Knives, of all possible challengers. The uneasy head is prey to his own imagination. 'In the night imagining some fear/How easy is a Bush supposed a Blair' – A Midsummer Nightmare.[1]

KING RICHARD: Stand all apart. Cousin of Buckingham –

BUCKINGHAM: My gracious sovereign?

KING RICHARD: Give me thy hand.
Sound
Here he ascendeth the throne
Thus high, by thy advice
And thy assistance, is King Richard seated.
But shall we wear these glories for a day?
Or shall they last, and we rejoice in them?

BUCKINGHAM: Still live they, and for ever let them last!

KING RICHARD: Ah, Buckingham, now do I play the touch,
To try if thou be current gold indeed.
Young Edward lives. Think now what I would speak.

BUCKINGHAM: Say on, my loving lord.

KING RICHARD: Why, Buckingham, I say I would be king.

BUCKINGHAM: Why, so you are, my thrice-renownèd lord.

KING RICHARD: Ha! Am I king? 'Tis so. But Edward lives.

BUCKINGHAM: True, noble prince.

KING RICHARD: O bitter consequence
That Edward still should live true noble prince!
Cousin, thou wast not wont to be so dull.
Shall I be plain? I wish the bastards dead,
And I would have it suddenly performed.
What sayst thou now? Speak suddenly, be brief.

BUCKINGHAM: Your grace may do your pleasure.

KING RICHARD: Tut, tut, thou art all ice; thy kindness freezes.
Say, have I thy consent that they shall die?

BUCKINGHAM: Give me some little breath, some pause,
                                                    dear lord,
Before I positively speak in this.
I will resolve you herein presently.
(Act IV.2)

The 'deep-revolving, witty Buckingham', the Mandelson of his day,
so skilled and adept at manipulating, suddenly fails to spot the
strategically-placed banana skin, not only failing to step over it but
hypnotised into placing his foot slap bang in the middle. The fickle,
chameleon mind of the serial killer knows no rest, owes no loyalty:

I will converse with iron-witted fools
And unrespective boys. None are for me
That look into me with considerate eyes.
High-reaching Buckingham grows circumspect.
(Act IV.2)

Richard is on the way down. Every move now will be an attempt to
defend his position. The Macbethian bear chained to the stake. The
retention of the crown now becomes the imperative, all thought of
governing abandoned. It is inevitable that he will look for omens where he
once gave the finger to fate. Claudius too becomes politically paralysed in
the face of Hamlet's idiosyncrasy. The man who murdered his brother in
order to take over the defence of the country – setting it on a war footing,
initiating an immediate twenty-four-hour round-the-clock arms race – is
strategically enfeebled by fear. Brutus on the eve of Philippi conjures up a
vision of the murdered Caesar. Richard, on the eve of the Battle of
Bosworth, summons up the lot – Anne, Clarence, the Princes, Rivers,
Vaughan, Grey, Buckingham all those he's done away with. We know he's
going to lose; it's not just a question of the sun not shining, in his head he's
already blown it. Funny how ghosts always appear at the right

psychological moment. They never turn up when we're having a good time – always seem to know when we're on a downer.

> Give me another horse! Bind up my wounds!
> Have mercy, Jesu! – Soft! I did but dream.
> O coward conscience, how dost thou afflict me!
> The lights burn blue. It is now dead midnight.
> Cold fearful drops stand on my trembling flesh.
> What do I fear? Myself? There's none else by.
> Richard loves Richard: that is, I am I.
> Is there a murderer here? No. Yes, I am.
> Then fly. What, from myself? Great reason why –
> Lest I revenge. Myself upon myself?
> Alack, I love myself. Wherefore? For any good
> That I myself have done unto myself?
> O no! Alas, I rather hate myself
> For hateful deeds committed by myself.
> I am a villain. Yet I lie, I am not.
> Fool, of thyself speak well. Fool, do not flatter.
> My conscience hath a thousand several tongues,
> And every tongue brings in a several tale,
> And every tale condemns me for a villain.
> Perjury, perjury, in the highest degree.
> Murder, stern murder, in the direst degree,
> All several sins, all used in each degree,
> Throng to the bar, crying all 'Guilty! Guilty!
> I shall despair. There is no creature loves me;
> And if I die, no soul will pity me.
> Nay, wherefore should they, since that I myself
> Find in myself no pity to myself?
> Methought the souls of all that I had murdered
> Came to my tent, and every one did threat
> Tomorrow's vengeance on the head of Richard.
> (Act V.3)

Fear of retribution in the next life? A crisis of identity? Throughout history the greatest tyrants and dictators have ultimately fallen prey to over-weaning megalomania to be found finally cowering in a hole – either real or imagined. But not before they have wreaked havoc. And once again, like Macbeth, Romeo, Hamlet, Richard reaches that moment of existential clarity where 'the readiness is all':

March on, join bravely, let us to't pell-mell,
If not to heaven, then hand in hand to hell.

Richard, in his action mode, prefigures modern western nihilism, a forerunner of Nietzsche's *Übermensch*, a man for whom morality is a word used to describe cowards, appeasers and religious rabbits. He is an early Eastwood, Schwarzenegger, Stallone, Cruise in *The Collector*, sending a *frisson* of excitement coursing through our veins. We wait for the villain to get his comeuppance, yet will him on to more and more outrageous deeds. He carries a public health warning, the Elizabethan equivalent of an over-18 certificate – at least he would, had we not become desensitised by the gratuitous violence that is now the staple diet on the small and large screen. Were the Elizabethans as sanguine about blood-letting as we are today? Casual slaughter, brutality, disease, inhumanity – the chances of survival into old age were slim. The opiate of religion or existential amorality? An unequal choice, really. Give me life in the here-and-now any day. For if history is no more than an unending, unbroken chain of gigantic slaughter, what remains except a leap into darkness, a world where no laws exist, a choice between death and pleasure, hedonism and pain? Richard III is Shakespeare's homage to Machiavelli. Politics for Richard is the art of acquiring power. Politics is amoral, something practical, akin to engineering, the skill that of the dazzling footwork of a Thiery Henri. Human emotions, people, are clay to be shaped at will. The whole world is there to be thrown on a wheel, producing a pot into which Richard will pour his ambition with a terrifying, ugly, cruel grin on his face. But Richard himself will in time become a lump of clay that another butcher will shape. As Jan Kott says, 'He who thought he was making history becomes himself the object of that history'.[2]

Power, for Shakespeare, is the crown. It is land. It is territory. It is people. But the value goes beyond the pecuniary worth. It is priceless.

The crown may be made of gold and heavy but it can be torn off a dying king's head and put on one's own. Then, merely by that one act, you're king. But either you wait until the king is dead or you do it for him (if Macbeth had waited he'd probably have been king anyway). Usurpation of the crown, fratricide, patricide, is a recurring Shakespearean theme. The history of slaughter is seemingly endless.

> **QUEEN MARGARET:** . . . I had an Edward, till a Richard
> killed him;
> I had a Harry, till a Richard killed him;
> Thou hadst an Edward, till a Richard killed him;
> Thou hadst a Ricahrd, till a Richard killed him.
>
> **DUCHESS OF YORK:** I had a Richard too, and thou didst
> kill him;
> I had a Rutland too, thou holp'st to kill him.
>
> **QUEEN MARGARET:** Thou hadst a Clarence too, and Richard
> killed him.
> From forth the kennel of thy womb hath crept
> A hellhound that doth hunt us all to death . . .
> . . . Thy Edward he is dead, that killed my Edward;
> Thy other Edward dead, to quit my Edward;
> Young York he is but boot, because both they
> Matched not the high perfection of my loss.
> Thy Clarence he is dead that stabbed my Edward,
> And the beholders of this frantic play,
> Th'adulterate Hastings, Rivers, Vaughan, Grey,
> Untimely smothered in their dusky graves.
> Richard yet lives, hell's black intelligencer;
> Only reserved their factor to buy souls
> And send th em thither . . .
> (Act IV.4)

Shakespearean tragedy, unlike Greek, is not a theatre of moral attitudes in the face of immortal gods. There are no fates, furies, supernatural forces that decide the hero's destiny. In the final analysis, this bare, forked animal is responsible for his own fate. The subject, object, result of the consequences of his own actions. The kings climb the Jan Kott staircase, his Grand Mechanism, pause briefly at the top to brandish a tarnished sword and then topple off, giving way to the next pretender, shuttling and shuffling his way up the moving staircase of history.

> . . . **There are no innocents . . . evil stems not from Richard but from a history he shares with others.**[3]

That history began at the dawn of English dynasty. Save for the princes in the Tower – guilty only by the association of the fact of their birth – all those eliminated by Richard bear the mark of present or earlier crimes. If Clarence and Edward are torn by remorse and guilt, they have reason to be. And if Margaret appears to be an instrument of fate, gloating over the downfall of others as one by one her prophesies come true, this is only a playwright's device for demonstrating the predictability of human greed when power is at stake. What is remarkable is the exactness of the fate assigned by Margaret to each one of Richard's victims:

> **Can curses pierce the clouds and enter heaven?**
> **Why then, give way, dull clouds, to my quick curses!**
> **Though not by war, by surfeit die your king,**
> **As ours by murder, to make him a king!**
> **Edward thy son, that now is Prince of Wales,**
> **For Edward our son, that was Prince of Wales,**
> **Die in his youth by like untimely violence!**
> **Thyself a queen, for me that was a queen,**
> **Outlive thy glory, like my wretched self!**
> **Long mayst thou live to wail thy children's death**
> **And see another, as I see thee now,**
> **Decked in thy rights as thou art stalled in mine!**
> **Long die thy happy days before thy death,**
> **And after many lengthened hours of grief,**
> **Die neither mother, wife, nor England's queen!**
> **Rivers and Dorset, you were standers-by,**

> And so wast thou, Lord Hastings, when my son
> Was stabbed with bloody daggers. God, I pray Him,
> That none of you may live his natural age,
> But by some unlooked accident cut off!
> (Act I.3)

Her predictions go off like time-bombs throughout the play. The escalating picture of horror that she paints seems to drive all sense of morality down a never-ending tunnel of darkness, a nightmare world of unending slaughter. Not much sign of God around, then. And having lived to see the cycle of violence eventually broken by Richmond, she returns from whence she came – to France, a catalyst yet a survivor of the bloodiest episode in Britain's civil history. Strange that she didn't spot Buckingham's downfall, though:

> O Princely Buckingham, I'll kiss thy hand
> In sign of league and amity with thee.
> Now fair befall thee and thy noble house!
> Thy garments are not spotted with our blood,
> Nor thou within the compass of my curse.
> (Act I.3)

Just shows that clairvoyance is an inexact science.

And what about Anne? Of what was she guilty? Marrying Richard in the first place. Much has been made of the fate of a young, defenceless girl, cast adrift in a world of sharks. What alternative had she to the offer of the hand of a powerful, charismatic figure? Well, she could have said no. In Shakespeare, girls do. But in one of the most remarkable seduction scenes in world drama, Richard literally woos her over the dead body of her dead father in law, seducing her at the very moment of her deepest hate.

> What though I killed her husband and her father?
> The readiest way to make the wench amends
> Is to become her husband and her father,
> The which will I – not all so much for love

As for another secret close intent
By marrying her which I must reach unto . . .
(Act I.1)

What dark subterranean sexual emotions did he awaken in her as his hand encompassed her breast? What black art of lust was unleashed in her young body to divert her so utterly from grieving? True, at moments of extreme emotion we are not always responsible for our responses but the awakening of desire in her at such a moment tells us more about Shakespeare's understanding of how sex drives our passions than all the acres of paper spent on Bill and Monica. 'Take up the sword again, or take up me' (Act I.2) Maybe she does have no choice. Unable to kill him in cold blood, Anne surrenders. But going off without a backward glance, his ring on her finger? And what is the 'secret close intent' to which Richard alludes? Having taken us completely into his confidence, sharing every thought and plan with us, why does he now withhold something from us in his relationship with Anne? Some political pimping afoot, with Anne as the sexual bait? A predilection for S and M? Maybe humping for Richard has a different connotation. Curious.

The two scenes involving the seduction of Anne and the attempted seduction of Elizabeth are the most remarkable in the play. In the latter, Richard attempts his tried and trusted technique on the young Elizabeth's mother. Another Plantagenet queen for his bed to bring forth yet more Plantagenets. Even Richard has one eye on his own mortality. Shakespeare often throws in a long verbal scene in Act IV, ostensibly to give the protagonist a cigarette break in the dressing room before the big fight in Act V: *Hamlet, Macbeth, Coriolanus*. But here Richard is still in action, doing verbal battle with a strong woman more than his equal:

QUEEN ELIZABETH: How canst thou woo her?

KING RICHARD: That would I learn of you,
As one being best acquainted with her humour.

QUEEN ELIZABETH: And wilt thou learn of me?

KING RICHARD: Madam, with all my heart.

QUEEN ELIZABETH: Send to her by the man that slew her brothers
A pair of bleeding hearts; thereon engrave
'Edward' and 'York'; then haply will she weep.
Therefore present to her – as sometimes Margaret
Did to thy father, steeped in Rutland's blood –
A handkerchief, which say to her did drain
The purple sap from her sweet brother's body,
And bid her wipe her weeping eyes withal.
If this inducement move her not to love,
Send her a letter of thy noble deeds:
Tell her thou mad'st away her uncle Clarence,
Her uncle Rivers; yea, and for her sake,
Mad'st quick conveyance with her good aunt Anne!

KING RICHARD: You mock me, madam; this is not the way
To win your daughter.
(Act IV.4)

Act IV.4 has ostensibly the same structure as Act I.2. Both follow the grieving for husbands, sons, daughters lost to Richard's death machine. Immediately prior to his entrance, Elizabeth has lamented the death of her two young sons. But where the scene with Anne was a striking demonstration of his powers, this is Richard's first big failure. The verbal thrust and parry is reminiscent of many a Shakespeare scene where the exchanges echo the dexterity of Elizabethan sword-play. Every attempt at forcing an opening is met with a reminder for Richard (and for us) of the litany of crimes he has committed. Mind you, it's a bit of a long shot trying to woo the mother of two young boys you've just done away with.

QUEEN ELIZABETH: What were I best to say? Her father's brother
Would be her lord? Or shall I say her uncle?
Or he that slew her brothers and her uncles?
Under what title shall I woo for thee
That God, the law, my honour, and her love
Can make seem pleasing to her tender years?

KING RICHARD: Infer fair England's peace by this alliance.

QUEEN ELIZABETH: Which she shall purchase with still-
                                             lasting war.

KING RICHARD: Tell her the King, that may command, entreats.

QUEEN ELIZABETH: That at her hands which the King's
                                             king forbids.

KING RICHARD: Say she shall be a high and mighty queen.

QUEEN ELIZABETH: To vail the title, as her mother doth.

KING RICHARD: Say I will love her everlastingly.

QUEEN ELIZABETH: But how long shall that title 'ever' last?

KING RICHARD: Sweetly in force unto her fair life's end.

QUEEN ELIZABETH: But how long fairly shall her sweet life last?

KING RICHARD: As long as heaven and nature lengthens it.

QUEEN ELIZABETH: As long as hell and Richard likes of it.

KING RICHARD: Say I, her sovereign, am her subject love.

QUEEN ELIZABETH: But she, your subject, loathes such
                                             sovereignty.

KING RICHARD: Be eloquent in my behalf to her.

QUEEN ELIZABETH: An honest tale speeds best being
                                             plainly told.

KING RICHARD: Then plainly to her tell my loving tale.

QUEEN ELIZABETH: Plain and honest is too harsh a style.

KING RICHARD: Your reasons are too shallow and too quick.

**QUEEN ELIZABETH: O no, my reasons are too deep and dead –
Too deep and dead, poor infants, in their graves.**

KING RICHARD: Harp not on that string, madam; that is past.

QUEEN ELIZABETH: Harp on it still shall I till heartstrings break.

Off she goes,

**QUEEN ELIZABETH: I go. Write to me very shortly,
And you shall understand from me her mind.**

KING RICHARD: Bear her my true love's kiss; and so farewell –

Exit Queen Elizabeth.

Relenting fool, and shallow, changing woman!

How should we be left? Does Elizabeth let him kiss her? If she does, is it a ploy to lure him into a false sense of security? 'Relenting fool and shallow changing woman'. Do we believe him? Is it necessary for the dramatic tension to believe he had a chance? We've already seen Anne succumb to his flattery. Is it tenable a second time so late in the play? I think not. And seeing Richard not believing it himself, even as he utters the words of contempt for her apparent reversal, leaves us tingling with anticipation as to how his final demise will be achieved. In the very next scene we learn that Elizabeth has offered her daughter to Richmond, thus cementing the Plantagenets and the Tudors, bringing a temporary pause in the hundred years of civil mayhem in the name of Divine Right. The Wars of the Roses are at an end. Not for another hundred and fifty years would Briton fight Briton, and then it was yet again to break the stranglehold of the royal family on the ruling of the country. But this time the cause was Republicanism. Oliver Cromwell. What a pity he failed. Maybe it was an act of God . . .

* * *

Notes

1. Misquote from A Midsummer Nights Dream, 'In the night imagining some fear/How easy is a bush supposed a bear', Act V.1
2. *Shakespeare Our Contemporary*, Jan Kott.
3. *The Dark Generations of Richard III, Criticism 1*, Murray Krieger 1959.

Appendices

Appendix I

LADY MORTIMER: *(weeping)*
Pied mynd I ryfela, f'anwylyd,
(Go not to these wars, my love)
Pied mynd I gyflafan ddisynnwyr a ladd gariad ieuanc
(Go not to the senseless slaughter of a love that is young)
sym or ddi rodres a ieuenctid ei hunan.
(And green as youth itself)
Pied mynd I refela!
(Go not to these wars!)

MORTIMER: This is the deadly spite that angers me;
My wife can speak no English, I no Welsh.

GLENDOWER: My daughter weeps: she will not part with you;
She'll be a soldier too, she'll to the wars.

MORTIMER: Good father, tell her that she and my aunt Percy
Shall follow in your conduct speedily.

GLENDOWER: Pied gofidio, fy merch, cei di a'th
(Do not worry girl, you and your)
Chwaer-yng-nghyfraith ddilyn eich cariadon.
(Sister-in-law can follow your loves)

LADY MORTIMER: Dilyn? I'r rhyfel?
(Follow? To the war?)

GLENDOWER: Cewch fod gyda nhw iw diddanu a'u.
(You may go with them to comfort them)
hanog yng nghanol y frwydr.
(And cheer them on in battle)

LADY MORTIMER: Cenedl ydym yn gwastraffu ein bywydau

in meistri
(We are a nation wasting ourselves)
Mewn rhyfeloedd ofer,
(In fruitless battles for our masters)
Mewn tiroedd nad oes gennym hawl arnynt
(In lands to which we have no claim)
Gyda dynion nad ydym yn eu casau
(With men for whom we feel no hatred)
Pied mynd I ryfela!
(Go not to these wars!)

GLENDOWER: She is desperate here; a peevish self-wind harlotry,
One that no persuasion can do good upon.
Fy merch, daw dim daioni o'r anfodlonrwydd yma!
(My girl, no good will come of this reluctance!)

LADY MORTIMER: Fy nhad, mae dyn un anferth dros fud bychan
(Father, man is huge in a small world)
Yn ei dywylly a'i falchder
(Overshadowed by his pride)

GLENDOWER: Dere 'ma, Catrin fach
(Come here, Catrin bach)
Rhoeddem yn genedl, acydym eto, pan
(We are a nation still, and when)
rhown heibio gweryla am friwsion o dan
(we have finished grovelling for crumbs)
fwrdd gnoi esgyrn diwilliant
(under the table or gnawing)
diflanedig. Ail atgyfodwn eto, wedi ein
(on the bones of a dead culture, we will arise, armed)
harfogi. Ond nid, dwi'n gobeithio, o dan yr hen drefn.
(armed. But not in the old way)
Cofia ddeall, Catrin Fach, 'na i gyd.
(Try to understand, Catrin Bach, that's all)

LADY MORTIMER: Annwylyd.

(My love)

Carcharwyd fi hyd nes y dathost ataf,

(I was in prison until you came)

Dy lais oedd yr allwedd a agorodd y

(Your voice was a key turning)

Clo anferth i anobaith. A agorodd y

(in the enormous lock of hopelessness)

drws i'm gollwng i neu dy adael

(Did the door open to let me out)

Di i mewn?

(Or you in)

MORTIMER: I understand thy looks that pretty Welsh
Which thou pour'st down from these swelling heavens
I am too perfect in, and, but for shame,
In such a parley should I answer thee.

LADY MORTIMER: Does dim amser i fwu a llai i farw, felly

(No time there is for life and even less)

Gyda'm holl ewllys ond yn erbyn

(For death. So with my whole will)

Dymuniad fy nghalon, ymwahanwn ein

(But against the wishes of my heart)

Dau yn awr,

(We'll separate now)

MORTIMER: I understand thy kisses and thou mine,
And that's a feeling disputation:
But I will never be a truant, love,
Till I have learned thy language, for thy tongue
Makes Welsh as sweet as ditties highly penn'd,
Sung by a fair queen in a summer's bower,
With ravishing division, to her lute.

GLENDOWER: Nay, if you melt, then will she run mad.
Dyna ddigion, fymerth cana, cana i mi

(Enough, girl, daughter sing, sing for me)

LADY MORTIMER: Rho dy ben, f'anwylyd, ar fy nghol a
(Lay your head my love, in my lap)
Chanaf gan i leddfu dy fryd anesmwyth.
(And I'll sing to soothe your troubled mind)

MORTIMER: O, I am ignorance itself in this!

GLENDOWER: She bids you rest your gentle head upon her lap,
And she will sing the song that pleaseth you
And those musicians that shall play to you
Hang in the air a thousand leagues from hence,
And straight they shall be here: sit, and attend.

Appendix II

The Ballad Of Harry Le Roy

Come all you good people who would hear a song
Of men bold and men brave, of men weak and men strong;
Of a king who was mighty but wild as a boy,
And list to the ballad of Harry Le Roy.

Of a King who was mighty but wild as a boy,
And list to the ballad of Harry Le Roy.

Thirteen ninety and eight is the year we begin,
King Richard the Second the reign we are in;
Two Lords fought a duel one bright summer's day,
Henry Bolingbroke of Lancaster and Thomas Mowbray.

Of a King who was mighty but wild as a boy,
And list to the ballad of Harry Le Roy.

Both mounted with lances on fire for the fight
Their horses a-flame, brave knight against knight
'Stop the joust' called King Richard, at the very last breath,
'Henceforth you're both exiled upon pain of death.'

Of a King who was mighty but wild as a boy,
And list to the ballad of Harry Le Roy.

One year passes by, Henry Bolingbroke returns,
At the head of an army for vengeance he burns
Defeats and imprisons King Richard alone,
Then murders him shamefully, seizes the throne.

Of a King who was mighty but wild as a boy,
And list to the ballad of Harry Le Roy.

Michael Bogdanov
Shakespeare Productions

1970/1

Assistant Director Royal Shakespeare Company (RSC) to John Barton, Terry Hands, Trevor Nunn, David Jones, Robin Phillips, Peter Brook (A Midsummer Nights Dream - Associate Director on World Tour).

1971

Two Gentleman of Verona (Os Dos Cabelleros di Verona). Tearto Ruth Escobar, Sao Paulo Brazil.

1972

The Tempest, Newcastle Playhouse. Designer – Stephanie Howard. Prospero – Bill Wallis.

1974

Twelfth Night, The Phoenix Theatre, Leicester. Designer - Mike Bearwish. Olivia – Heather Sears. Orsino – Darryl Forbes-Dawson.

1974

Romeo and Juliet, Haymarket Theatre, Leicester. Designer – Adrian Vaux. Romeo – Jonathan Kent. Juliet – Mary Rutherford. Mercutio – Bill Wallis. Paris – Alan Rickman.

1975

Hamlet, The Phoenix Theatre, Leicester. Designer – Paul Bannister. Hamlet – Hugh Thomas. Claudius – Bill Wallis.

1975

'He That Plays the King' Trilogy; Richard III, Hamlet, The Tempest. The Phoenix Theatre, Leicester. Designer – Paul Bannister. Hamlet, Prospero & Richard III – Bill Wallis.

1978

The Taming of the Shrew, RSC, Stratford. Designer — Chris Dyer. Petruchio — Jonathan Pryce. Katherina — Paula Dionissotti. Grumio — David Suchet. Tranio — Ian Charleson. Bianca — Zoe Wannamaker.

1979

Hamlet, The Tempest, Richard III — The 'Action Man' Trilogy, The Young Vic Theatre. Designer — Paul Bannister. Hamlet — Phil Bowen. Richard III & Prospero — Bill Wallis.

1979

The Taming of the Shrew — RSC, The Aldwych Theatre, London. Cast as before. Society of West End Theatres (SWET) Director of the Year Award.

1980

The 'Action Man' Trilogy, The Old Vic Theatre, London. Hamlet — Tony Milner. Richard III & Prospero — Bill Wallis.

1982

Macbeth, The National Theatre Educational Touring Production. Macbeth — Greg Hicks.

1983

Romeo and Juliet, The Imperial Theatre, Tokyo, Japan. Designer — Chris Dyer.

1984

Hamlet, The Abbey Theatre, Dublin. Designer — Juliet Watkinson. Hamlet — Stephen Brennan.

1985

Measure for Measure, The Stratford Memorial Theatre, Ontario, Canada. Designer — Chris Dyer. The Duke — Alan Scarfe.

1986

Julius Ceaser, The Deutsches Shauspielhaus, Hamburg (The National

Theatre). Designer – Chris Dyer. Brutus – Michel Degen. Cassius – Dietrich Mattausch. Antony – Uli Tukur.

1986

The Henrys, The English Shakespeare Company (ESC). Designers – Chris Dyer & Stephanie Howard. Hal, Henry V - Michael Pennington. Falstaff – John Woodvine.

1986

Romeo & Juliet, RSC. Designer – Chris Dyer. Romeo – Sean Bean. Juliet - Naimh Cusack. Mercutio – Michael Kitchen. Tybalt – Hugh Quarshie.

1987

Romeo & Juliet, The Barbican Theatre, London. Cast – as before.

1987 – 1989

The Wars of the Roses, English Shakespeare Company World Tour. Designers – Chris Dyer & Stephanie Howard. Richard II, Hal, Henry V – Michael Penningon. Henry VI – Paul Brennan. Richard III – Andrew Jarvis. Falstaff – Barry Stanton. Laurence Olivier Award for Best Director.

1989

Hamlet, The Deutsches Schauspielhaus, Hamburg. Designer – Bill Dudley. Hamlet – Uli Tukur. Claudius – Christian Redl. Gertrude – Ilse Ritter.

1990

Romeo & Juliet, The Deutsches Shauspielhaus, Hamburg. Designer – Chris Dyer. Romeo – Marcus Blum. Juliet – Caterina Striebeck. Tybalt – Hugh Quarshie.

1990

Coriolanus and The Winter's Tale, The ESC World Tour. Designers – Chris Dyer and Claire Lyth. Corialanus/Leontes – Michael Pennington (TMA Best touring Production).

1991

The Tempest, The Deutsches Schauspielhaus, Hamburg. Designer —Chris Dyer. Prospero — Uli Wildgruber.

1992

Macbeth, ESC. Designer — Claire Lyth. Macbeth — Michael Pennington. Lady Macbeth — Jenny Quayle.

1992

Macbeth, ESC;a landrover tour of Sierra Leone, Ghana, Namibia, Malawi - Africa. Designer — Claire Lyth.

1992

Macbeth & The Tempest, ESC World Tour. Macbeth — Tony Haygarth. Lady Macbeth — Lynne Farleigh. Prospero — John Woodvine.

1994

Romeo & Juliet, ESC. Designer — Chris Dyer. Romeo — Jo Dixon. Juliet — Joanna Roth.

1997

Timon of Athens. The Chicago Shakespeare Theatre, Chicago. Designer — Ralph Koltai. Timon — Larry Yando.

1997

Macbeth, Bayerisches Staatsschauspiel in Munich. Designer — Claire Lyth. Macbeth — Uli Tukur.

1998

Anthony & Cleopatra and As You Like It, ESC, Bath Shakespeare Festival. Designers — Geraldine Bunzl & Yannis Thavoris. Anthony — Tim Woodward. Cleopatra — Cathy Tyson. Rosalind — Ivy Omere.

2000

Troilus & Cressida, The Bell Shakespeare Company for the Olympic Arts Festival, Sydney Opera House, Australia. Designer — Michael Scott-Mitchell & Ulrike Engelbrecht. Troilus- Toby Truslove, Cressida —

Blazey Best , Pandarus — Billie Brown.

2002
The Merry Wives of Windsor, Ludlow Festival. Designer — Chris Dyer. Falstaff — Philip Madoc.

2003
The Winter's Tale, Chicago Shakespeare Theatre, Chicago. Designers — Derek McClane and Claire Lyth. Leontes — John Reeger. Hermione — Barbara Robertson.

2003
The Merchant of Venice & The Winter's Tale, The Ludlow Festival. Designers — Chris Dyer & Mel Wing. Leontes — Russell Gomer. Hermione — Nickie Rainsford., Shylock — Philip Madoc. Portia — Heledd Baskerville.

2004
Cymbeline and Twelfth Night — The Ludlow Festival. Designers Ed Thomas and Sian Jenkins. Imogen — Nia Roberts, Cymbeline — John Labanowski, Malvolio — Paul Greenwood, Viola — Heledd Baskerville.

2004
Twelfth Night, Cymbeline, The Merchant of Venice — The Wales Theatre Company. Designers — Ed Thomas, Sean Crowley, Sian Jenkins. Malvolio — Paul Greenwood, Imogen — Lisa Zahra, Shylock — Philip Madoc.

2005
Hamlet — The Wales Theatre Company. Bi-lingual, back to back Welsh/English language production. Designers Ed Thomas & Sean Crowley. Hamlet Wayne Cater.

TV & Film

1982
Shakespeare Lives, Channel 4. Twelve part series live from the Roundhouse, London.

1987

Julius Ceaser, ZDF, Germany.

1990

The Wars of the Roses – The English Shakespeare Company 7 play History cycle. Portman Films.

1995

Shakespeare on the Estate, BBC Bard on the Box series. (Royal Television Society Award Best Documentary. BAFTA Nomination, Banff Film Festival Award Best Documentary.

1996

The Tempest in Butetown – 90 minute feature film for BBC with the residents of Tiger Bay, Cardiff.

1997

Macbeth, Granada – Channel 4. Macbeth – Sean Pertwee. Lady Macbeth – Greta Scacci. Malcolm – Jack Davenport. Banquo – Michael Maloney.

2004

The Welsh in Shakespeare, BBC 60 minute drama documentary with Michael Sheen, Philip Madoc, Mark Lewis Jones.

Shakespeare: The Director's Cut
Michael Bogdanov

This collection of cutting-edge essays is a valuable addition to Shakespeare studies, and to theatre studies more generally. Michael Bogdanov's cuts are always incisive, razor-sharp, and applied with an unerring hand. Never dogmatic or programmatic, Bogdanov approaches each play attentive to its novelty and its nuances, alive to its urgency and impact, attuned to its language and its lore. As a director acutely aware of critical conventions - enough to want to overturn them - Bogdanov is uniquely positioned to combine theoretical acuity with a practitioner's knowledge of what works on the page and in performance, while never losing sight of what is most politically resonant and socially engaged. The meat is moist closest to the bone, and these are choice cuts from a master butcher.

**Willy Maley, Professor of Renaissance Studies,
University of Glasgow**

For 30 years Michael Bogdanov has been the most consistently interesting and provocative of British directors of Shakespeare. Now he has written a series of incisive essays on the plays - not comments on his many productions, but introductions to the works that show the result of his long acquaintance with them. The essays, based in social thought and theatrical savvy, make Shakespeare accessible and immediate and will be of interest to a wide range of readers.

**Dennis Kennedy, Beckett Professor of Drama,
Trinity College Dublin**

Michael Bogdanov is the Tyrone Guthrie of our day, and his signature is all over the work of many young directors. He is at once scholar, provocateur, puritan and Lord of Misrule.

Michael Pennington

ISBN 0-9545206-0-2

£8.99

Available from Booksource
Tel: +44(0)8702 402 182 Fax: +44(0)141 557 0189
email: orders@booksource.net

Available from all major bookshops, amazon.co.uk and
www.capercailliebooks.co.uk.

Understanding Anti-Americanism
Its Impact and Origin
Edited by Paul Hollander

Paul Hollander is professor emeritus of sociology at the University of Massachusetts, Amherst, USA and author of the classic *Anti-Americanism* as well as *Political Will and Personal Belief*, *Decline and Discontent*, *The Many Faces of Socialism* and *Political Pilgrims*.

America is hardly perfect, but what accounts for the gush of virulent criticism, known as anti-Americanism, emanating from America's friends or America itself as well as its enemies? Paul Hollander leads a distinguished team of scholars in an examination, both vigorous and detached, from all aspects of the problem. A serious, comprehensive book, relevant for today.

> **Harvey Mansfield, Professor of Government,**
> **Harvard University**

A fascinating collection of essays on a complex but important topic by some of America's foremost scholars and thinkers.

> **Robert Kagan, Senior Associate at the Carnegie**
> **Endowment for International Peace**

What the 18 assembled authors conclude is both fascinating and depressing. Hollander has performed a great service with this volume.

> **National Review**

ISBN 0-9549625-7-5

£10.99

Available from Booksource
Tel: +44(0)8702 402 182 Fax: +44(0)141 557 0189
email: orders@booksource.net

Available from all major bookshops, amazon.co.uk and
www.capercailliebooks.co.uk.

Six contemporary plays by Capercaillie Books

Blooded by Isabel Wright
ISBN 0-9549625-4-0

Dissent by Stephen Greenhorn
ISBN 0-9545206-9-6

Electra by Tom McGrath
ISBN 0-9549625-2-4

Oedipus The Visionary by David Greig
ISBN 0-9549625-1-6

Opium Eater by Andrew Dallmeyer
ISBN 0-9549625-3-2

The Salt Wound by Stephen Greenhorn
ISBN 0-9549625-0-8

£8.99

Available from Booksource
Tel: +44(0)8702 402 182 Fax: +44(0)141 557 0189
email: orders@booksource.net

Web orders at www.capercailliebooks.co.uk

Other plays published by Capercaillie Books

Dr Korczak's Example by David Greig
ISBN 0-9545206-1-0

Kaahini by Maya Chowdhry
ISBN 0-9545206-4-5

King Matt by Stephen Greenhorn
ISBN 0-9545206-2-9

The Life of Stuff by Simon Donald
ISBN 0-9545206-6-1

Sunburst Finish by Andrea Gibb and Paddy Cunneen
ISBN 0-9545206-5-3

The Waltzer by Rhiannon Tise
ISBN 0-9545206-3-7

£5.99 each

Available from Booksource
Tel: +44(0)8702 402 182 Fax: +44(0)141 557 0189
email: orders@booksource.net

Web orders at www.capercailliebooks.co.uk